Combatting Eutrophication in the Baltic Sea: Legal Aspects of Sea-Based Engineering Measures

The Law of the Sea

Editors-in-Chief

Donald R. Rothwell (*Australian National University*)
Davor Vidas (*Fridtjof Nansen Institute*)

Associate Editors

Aldo Chircop (*Dalhousie University*)
David Freestone (*The George Washington University*)
Elizabeth Kirk (*University of Dundee*)
James Kraska (*U.S. Naval War College*)
Seokwoo Lee (*Inha University*)
Nilufer Oral (*Istanbul Bilgi University; Member, International Law Commission*)
Irini Papanicolopulu (*University of Milan-Bicocca*)
Karen Scott (*University of Canterbury*)
Tullio Treves (*University of Milan; former Judge of the
International Tribunal for the Law of the Sea*)
Seline Trevisanut (*Utrecht University*)

Volumes published in this Brill Research Perspectives title are listed at *brill.com/rpls*

Combatting Eutrophication in the Baltic Sea: Legal Aspects of Sea-Based Engineering Measures

Legal Perspectives

By

Henrik Ringbom
Brita Bohman
Saara Ilvessalo

BRILL

LEIDEN | BOSTON

This paperback book edition is simultaneously published as issue 2.4 (2018) of *Law of the Sea*, DOI:10.1163/24519359-12340007.

Library of Congress Control Number: 2019947503

Typeface for the Latin, Greek, and Cyrillic scripts: "Brill". See and download: brill.com/brill-typeface

ISBN 978-90-04-39956-3 (paperback)
ISBN 978-90-04-39957-0 (e-book)

Copyright 2019 by Henrik Ringbom, Brita Bohman and Saara Ilvessalo. Published by Koninklijke Brill NV, Leiden, The Netherlands.
Koninklijke Brill NV incorporates the imprints Brill, Brill Hes & De Graaf, Brill Nijhoff, Brill Rodopi, Brill Sense, Hotei Publishing, mentis Verlag, Verlag Ferdinand Schöningh and Wilhelm Fink Verlag.
Koninklijke Brill NV reserves the right to protect the publication against unauthorized use and to authorize dissemination by means of offprints, legitimate photocopies, microform editions, reprints, translations, and secondary information sources, such as abstracting and indexing services including databases. Requests for commercial re-use, use of parts of the publication, and/or translations must be addressed to Koninklijke Brill NV.

This book is printed on acid-free paper and produced in a sustainable manner.

Contents

Combatting Eutrophication in the Baltic Sea: Legal Aspects of Sea-Based Engineering Measures   1
> *Henrik Ringbom, Brita Bohman and Saara Ilvessalo*

Abstract   1

Keywords   2

1   Introduction   2
   1.1   *Background*   2
   1.2   *Outline and Structure of the Study*   5

2   Applicable Legal Framework for Sea-Based Measures   7
   2.1   *General*   7
   2.2   *Global Rules*   7
      2.2.1   The UN Convention on the Law of the Sea   7
         2.2.1.1   *Sea-Based Measures and the Zonal Approach of UNCLOS*   7
         2.2.1.2   *Obligations to Protect and Preserve the Marine Environment*   11
      2.2.2   The London Convention and the London Protocol   14
      2.2.3   The Convention on Biological Diversity   16
   2.3   *Regional Rules*   17
      2.3.1   The Helsinki Convention   17
         2.3.1.1   *General*   17
         2.3.1.2   *Provisions of Relevance for Sea-Based Measures*   19
      2.3.2   EU Laws for Water and Marine Environment   22
         2.3.2.1   *General*   22
         2.3.2.2   *The EU Marine Strategy Framework Directive and the Water Framework Directive*   23
         2.3.2.3   *The Marine Spatial Planning Directive*   24
      2.3.3   Other EU Instruments   25
         2.3.3.1   *The Habitats Directive and the Birds Directive*   25
         2.3.3.2   *The Waste Framework Directive*   26
      2.3.4   Assessment   27
         2.3.4.1   *The Role of the Marine Directives*   27
         2.3.4.2   *The* Weser *Case*   29
         2.3.4.3   *The Application of the* Weser *Case to Marine Strategy Framework Directive*   31

CONTENTS

2.4 *Environmental Impact Assessments* 32
   2.4.1 The Espoo Convention 32
   2.4.2 The EIA Directive 35
2.5 *Legal Categorization and Definition of Sea-Based Measures* 36
   2.5.1 General 36
   2.5.2 Dredging of Phosphorus-Rich Sediment 36
   2.5.3 Chemical Treatment 38
   2.5.4 Oxygenation 42
2.6 *Summary* 45

3 Key Issues Raised by Sea-Based Measures 47
3.1 *General* 47
3.2 *Convergence of Concerns: Regulatory Relevance* 48
   3.2.1 The Duty to Protect the Marine Environment 48
   3.2.2 Could Sea-Based Measures be Characterized as Pollution? 50
   3.2.3 Long-Term vs Short-Term Environmental Effects 52
3.3 *Dealing with Uncertainties: the Role of Environmental Principles* 54
   3.3.1 Relevant Environmental Law Principles 54
   3.3.2 The Precautionary Principle 57
   3.3.3 Addressing Geoengineering Measures at the London Dumping Regime – a Relevant Example? 59
3.4 *Summary* 63

4 The Relevance and Role of National Law 65
4.1 *Two Examples of National Legislation: Finland and Sweden* 65
4.2 *The Permit Procedure* 67
   4.2.1 Introduction 67
   4.2.2 The Finnish Permit System 67
      4.2.2.1 *Environmental Permit* 67
      4.2.2.2 *Permit under the Water Act* 70
      4.2.2.3 *Implementation of the Water Framework Directive* 72
      4.2.2.4 *Summary* 74
   4.2.3 The Swedish Permit System 75
      4.2.3.1 *General Procedural Provisions for Sea-Based Measures* 76
      4.2.3.2 *Permits for Hazardous Activities* 78
      4.2.3.3 *Environmental Quality Standards and the Implementation of the WFD* 78
      4.2.3.4 *Summary* 79
4.3 *Conclusion on the Role of National Procedures* 79

CONTENTS VII

5 Recent Development at HELCOM 81
6 Concluding Observations 84
    6.1 *On the Legal Position of Sea-Based Measures* 84
    6.2 *Observations Relating to Regulatory Voids* 85
    6.3 *On the Way Ahead* 87
List of References 88
Authors' Biographical Notes 95

Combatting Eutrophication in the Baltic Sea: Legal Aspects of Sea-Based Engineering Measures

Henrik Ringbom
Scandinavian Institute of Maritime Law, University of Oslo, Norway,
and Åbo Akademi University, Turku, Finland
henrik.ringbom@abo.fi

Brita Bohman
University of Gothenburg and Stockholm University, Sweden
brita.bohman@juridicum.su.se

Saara Ilvessalo
Baltic Area Legal Studies BALEX, Turku, Finland
saara.ilvessalo@centrumbalticum.org

Abstract

The main environmental problem of the Baltic Sea is that too many nutrients are being released to the sea (eutrophication). As many of the 'easy' measures to reduce the load from land-based sources have been put in place, increasing attention is given to measures to reduce the release of nutrients from the seabed sediments through the use of various technologies at sea, i.e. 'sea-based' measures.

There is no specific legal framework available for sea-based measures, but a number of provisions set general obligations to protect and preserve the marine environment.

The analysis indicates that neither the type of measure nor the geographical location of the activity is of decisive importance for the legal rights and obligations involved. Instead, the legality of any sea-based measure depends on the risks they present balanced against their benefits. There is considerable uncertainty on all these issues, and the matter is further complicated by the fact that both the risks and the benefits of the measures relate to their environmental impact.

It is recommended that a regional risk-based framework is established for assessing when and how further research on sea-based technologies can be undertaken in the Baltic Sea.

© HENRIK RINGBOM, BRITA BOHMAN & SAARA ILVESSALO, 2019 | DOI:10.1163/9789004399570_002

Keywords

Baltic Sea environmental protection – Baltic Marine Environment Protection Commission (HELCOM) – eutrophication – sea-based measures – marine geoengineering – precautionary principle – environmental impact assessment – Finland – Sweden – national permit regulations

1 Introduction

1.1 *Background*

The Baltic Sea is unique in many ways, due to its geographical, ecological and governance characteristics. The principal environmental threat facing the Baltic Sea, eutrophication, is also relatively unique, partly due to these characteristics. Eutrophication is the result of excessive inputs of nutrients, mainly phosphorus and nitrogen, into the sea, from a variety of sources, including industries, agriculture and waste water. These nutrients stimulate the growth of aquatic plant life. Yet overgrowth of plants and algae blocks sunlight and, in the degradation phase, consumes the oxygen of the sea thereby contributing to a state of hypoxia.[1] The Baltic Sea is also a semi-enclosed sea area with limited water exchange, which means that very limited quantities of oxygenized water from surrounding seas reach the central parts of the Baltic Sea.[2] The lack of oxygen at the bottom of the sea, in turn, initiates a chemical process whereby phosphorus (from historic excess inputs) that is tied to the seabed sediments is released, thereby causing another source of nutrients in the sea.[3]

The eutrophication and resulting oxygen depletion is connected to, and accelerates, a series of other environmental problems in the Baltic Sea. Hypoxia affects the entire marine ecosystem and large parts of the seabed is now considered dead, with no animal or plant life in these areas.[4]

---

1 See, e.g. Vahanen Environment Oy and Centrum Balticum, *Speeding up the Ecological Recovery of the Baltic Sea* (Ministry of the Environment of Finland, Helsinki: 2018) 29–31, https://vahanen.com/app/uploads/2018/05/Speeding_up_the_ecological_recovery_of_the_Baltic_Sea.pdf, (accessed 10.01.2019).

2 R. Elmgren, 'Understanding Human Impact on the Baltic Ecosystem: Changing Views in Recent Decades' in *Man and the Baltic Sea* (Ambio, Vol. 30, No. 4/5, 2001) 222.

3 Vahanen Environment Oy and Centrum Balticum, 2018, 29–31.

4 U. Larsson, R. Elmgren, and F. Wulff, *Eutrophication and the Baltic Sea: Causes and Consequences* (Ambio, Vol. 14, No. 1: 1985) 10; B. G. Gustafsson, et al., *Reconstructing the Development of Baltic Sea Eutrophication 1850–2006* (Ambio, Vol. 41: 2013) generally.

COMBATTING EUTROPHICATION IN THE BALTIC SEA

In terms of mitigation, a broad range of initiatives have been taken to deal with eutrophication of the Baltic Sea over the past decades. As much of the 'low-hanging fruit' in terms of sewage treatment plants, wastewater reductions, and other land-based measures to reduce nutrient input into the sea has already been harvested, attention is increasingly turned to new forms of reduction measures, including technological innovations that could be implemented at sea to target the phosphorus leakage from the seabed.

The measures that are currently envisaged can be broadly grouped into three main categories: those focusing on removal of the phosphorus-rich parts of the sediments (through dredging or 'skimming'), those influencing the chemical composition of the sediments through the treatment of the seabed with chemicals, and those seeking to improve oxygen levels in the seabed through different forms of oxygenation processes (notably by pumping oxygen-rich surface water down to the bottom). For reasons of convenience the three categories are generally referred to as 'dredging', 'chemical treatment' and 'oxygenation' below.

It is obvious that a large spectrum of measures and technologies fit into these categories and that the sea-based measures differ widely in technology, effect and availability. Not all of them are suitable for all sea areas or all scales of deployment – several of them are not even technically ready to deploy yet. The different types of measures involve different risks and challenges, but generally speaking, measures of this kind have been met with considerable scepticism from environmental scientists who highlight the risk of further deteriorating the state of the environment. In the opinion of these scientists, there are no 'quick-fixes' as alternatives to land-based emission limitations, which are proven to work, albeit very slowly.[5]

The states around the Baltic Sea have shown a significant divergence in their policy attitudes towards sea-based measures. When it comes to the general state-level acceptance and interest in adopting sea-based measures as a method to reduce eutrophication, the impression is that there is considerable reluctance among several HELCOM states. Only Sweden and Finland are openly positive towards taking such measures, as a supplement to land-based measures, and about exploring how this openness could be translated into practice.[6] Other countries are less convinced, noting, *inter alia*, that land-based

---

5 Minutes from the seminar "*Sea-based Measures – to Reduce Consequences of Eutrophication*", held at Stockholm University 12 February 2015, organized by Stockholm University, SWAM and the Swedish Ministry of Environment and Energy.

6 HELCOM HOD 50-2016, *OUTCOME of the 50th Meeting of the Heads of Delegation*, Agenda Item 4, (4.64); HELCOM Pressure 6-2017, *A joint HELCOM-EUSBSR workshop on internal*

measures are not yet exhausted as a mechanism to reduce nutrient inputs into the Baltic Sea. Even the majority of the organizations that see the potential merits of sea-based measures have emphasized that reducing the external nutrient load should still be the principal way to reduce eutrophication. The EU has not provided an official policy regarding eutrophication measures, but through its Strategy for the Baltic Sea Region (EUSBSR) in its Policy Action Area 'Nutri', reference has been made to such measures.[7] A recent study on the policy attitudes towards sea-based measures indicates that the overall policy resistance towards these measures relates both to concerns about what risks such actions may pose to the ecosystem, as well as concerns about what such measures would implicate for the overall regulatory or policy approach for the choice of measures to combat eutrophication.[8]

The principal aim of this study is to analyze the legal framework that applies to sea-based measures. In the absence of a specific legal framework in place for such measures, the matter is governed by a number of more generic international, EU-wide and national obligations and principles related to marine environmental protection. Their application raises a series of interesting legal questions relating to how sea-based measures should be classified and what rights and obligations apply to the various types of measures in different parts of the Baltic Sea.

At the same time, the topic also represents a case study for how international environmental law operates in the absence of specific regulation. What tools are there to ensure that the law keeps up with new scientific and technological developments? What happens when concrete questions are to be decided on the basis of generic rules and principles of environmental law, and how do those rules and principles operate in cases of scientific uncertainty about the consequences of the activity in question? How do different regulatory layers interact with each other in the absence of specific rules and are there any legal precedents to draw upon? The study addresses such questions, along with presenting recent regional efforts to fill the governance gap surrounding sea-based

---

   nutrient reserves, (7-10-Rev. 1), Agenda Item 7; HELCOM HOD 52–2017, *HELCOM-EUSBSR workshop on internal nutrient reserves*, (3-4), Agenda Item 3.

7   The EUSBSR was approved by the European Council in 2009 following a communication from the European Commission. The EUSBSR is implemented through concrete joint projects and processes in its different Policy Action Areas, and especially through so-called Flagship projects. So far, sea-based measures have not reached the status of a Flagship project, and thus only represent an 'Action Area' within the strategy. See actions 1 and 6 of *Policy area Nutri Actions at the EUSBRS Action Plan*, http://groupspaces.com/eusbsr-nutrient-inputs/pages/actions, (accessed 24.1.2019).

8   Vahanen Environment Oy and Centrum Balticum, 2018, 155.

measures, within the Baltic Marine Environment Protection Commission (Helsinki Commission, or HELCOM).

1.2 Outline and Structure of the Study

Part 2 describes the legal framework in which the sea-based measures operate. It briefly presents the main rules and principles of importance in international and EU law and assesses how sea-based measures situate in that framework. On the one hand, the absence of specific rules for sea-based measures means that a very broad range of international and EU environmental rules may be invoked for assessing their legality. The relevant rules range from procedural rules (relating to environmental impact assessments and permit procedures) and environmental principles (such as the precautionary principle and the best available technology) to a broad range of substantive rules covering issues such as marine environmental protection, biological diversity, dumping and marine geoengineering. The focus of the review is on rules of international law and EU law, which represent the substantive underpinning of the national rules in most Baltic Sea states (the most obvious exception being the Russian Federation that is not an EU member state). On the other hand, the absence of specific rules also means that the available rules and principles will not normally provide very precise answers to questions of direct implementation. It is also observed that EU law, in particular as interpreted in one or two key judgments by the Court of Justice of the European Union (CJEU), has affected this starting point, and introduced a new geographical differentiation which is based on other geographical criteria than those following from the law of the sea.

On this basis, section 2.5 categorizes different types of sea-based measures and identifies the applicable international laws, depending on what type of measure is at issue and in what sea area it operates. It is necessary to establish whether the existing legal framework covers such activities at all, whether analogies can be made to the regulation of comparable activities, or whether they remain to be governed only by more generic (environmental) legal principles. The three groups identified in section 2.5, and presented in a summarising table in section 2.6, invoke partially different legal questions and requirements, as do the different sea areas concerned. It turns out, however, that such a categorization is only partially decisive for determining the legal rights and obligations involved.

A more decisive element for establishing the legal position of sea-based measures relates to their impact on the marine environment. The environmental effects and risks of an activity will, for example, be decisive for determining whether the activity is to be considered 'pollution of the marine environment', 'dumping' or 'marine geoengineering', all of which are key concepts for determining the rights and obligations involved. A particular feature of sea-based measures is also that the risks that they involve and their purpose and assumed benefit relate to the same concern, i.e. the ecological well-being of the sea. This raises some questions relating to how certain key legal obligations operate in this context and to the weighing of the interests involved. Part 3 analyzes selected examples in more detail, concluding that the legality of sea-based measures is closely linked to whether or not they are effective in meeting their environmental objectives. This matter, in turn, is subject to significant scientific uncertainty.

Existing legal rules and principles, at all regulatory layers, are largely based upon the premise that information is available about technologies, alternatives, risks and consequences. Since this type of information is generally not available with respect to sea-based measures, the question as to how the law deals with scientific uncertainty becomes critical. Section 3.3 addresses some relevant principles that have been developed in international environmental law to this end, with a particular emphasis on the precautionary principle. Uncertainties surrounding the meaning and impact of these principles limit them as a tool for providing general guidance. The precautionary principle has not been operationalized at a regional level in a Baltic Sea context, but recent developments in the global regulation of geoengineering may well provide inspiration for how the matter could be approached at a regional level in the Baltic Sea region.

In view of the many legal uncertainties that exist in the international legal framework, a key role in the application and interpretation of the laws and principles will be held by national (or sub-national) authorities in charge of permits for such measures. It is at this level that the various interests involved will eventually be balanced against each other and the open-ended rules and principles will thus be applied and concretized. It is expected that all types of sea-based measures discussed in this article will require some form of permit, for any sea area concerned in the Baltic Sea. A more detailed review of the procedural requirements in two states, Finland and Sweden, is undertaken in Part 4. It transpires that at this level, too, there are few mechanisms in place to guide decision-makers whereby the technical and scientific knowledge surrounding the measures is incomplete or lacking.

The first steps towards operationalizing the precautionary principle for sea-based measures have recently been undertaken within HELCOM, where an interest has been expressed by the organization to develop guiding regional management principles and a risk assessment framework for the purpose. This development is briefly discussed in Part 5.

Part 6 finally offers some concluding remarks on the legal position of sea-based measures, on how international law, on the basis of this case study, handles legal voids and on how the governance of sea-based measures could be taken forward at a regional level.

2 Applicable Legal Framework for Sea-Based Measures

2.1 *General*

The first challenge concerning sea-based measures is how to situate them in the applicable legal framework. In the absence of rules that specifically govern these types of measures, it is necessary to establish whether the existing legal framework covers such activities at all, whether analogies can be made to the regulation of comparable activities, or whether they remain to be governed only by more generic (environmental) legal principles. This Part addresses that question, first in respect of the global marine environmental rules (section 2.2), and also in light of certain specific rules that apply regionally in the Baltic Sea through the Helsinki Convention (section 2.3.1). In addition, a very relevant group of requirements emanate from the EU marine directives (WFD and MSFD) and related case law, which may imply important restrictions for some or all of the sea-based measures discussed here (section 2.3.2). Sea-based measures may finally be subject to certain procedural rules at different regulatory levels, such as environmental impact assessments (EIAS) (section 2.4). On this basis, section 2.5 categorizes different types of sea-based measures and identifies the applicable international laws, depending on what type of measure is at issue and in what sea area it operates. Section 2.6 presents the categories and main applicable international rules in a tabular format.

2.2 *Global Rules*

2.2.1 The UN Convention on the Law of the Sea

2.2.1.1 *Sea-Based Measures and the Zonal Approach of UNCLOS*

The 1982 UN Convention on the Law of the Sea (UNCLOS) is the key international instrument – a universally applicable comprehensive framework convention seeking to regulate all activities in marine areas. All states in the Baltic Sea region and the EU are parties to the convention, which is widely regarded to be a 'Constitution for the Oceans' and representative of customary law, even for the states that have not formally ratified it.[9] It applies to any

---

9   See e.g. D. R. Rothwell and T. Stephens, *The International Law of the Sea*, Second ed. (Hart Publishing, Oxford/Portland: 2016) 23; Y. Tanaka, *The International Law of the Sea*, Second ed.

marine area, including those beyond the jurisdiction of any state, and also includes rules for delimiting sea areas.

In the case of the Baltic Sea, the maritime delimitation is nearly complete, i.e. the maritime borders are largely settled between the neighboring countries. Apart from a few delimitation points that are yet to be settled,[10] the entire Baltic Sea is divided between the coastal states and every part of it is subject to the jurisdiction of one of the coastal states. The 'high seas' areas of the Baltic Sea have thus disappeared in the process and there are no more 'no man's lands' in the Baltic Sea or its seabed. This state of affairs strengthens the picture – and jurisdictional reality – that questions related to the regulation and usage of the Baltic Sea and its resources are now for the Baltic Sea littoral states themselves to regulate and resolve. The maritime boundaries in the Baltic Sea are shown below: see Figure 1.

UNCLOS comprehensively regulates jurisdiction at sea, i.e. what states can and cannot do in different sea areas of the seabed and the water column, respectively. The jurisdictional principles of UNCLOS are based on the premise that flag states' jurisdiction is the same irrespective of the location of the activity in question, whereas coastal states' jurisdiction depends on the maritime zone concerned. The rules differ depending on what activity is concerned, but the principle for the seabed as well as the water column is that coastal states' jurisdiction over foreign ships and operators is larger in maritime areas near the coast and more limited in the Exclusive Economic Zone (EEZ).

In the EEZ, coastal states, on the one hand, have sovereign rights to perform activities with the purpose of exploring, exploiting, conserving, and managing the living as well as the non-living natural resources, and for the purpose of other activities for the economic exploitation and exploration of the zone.[11] On the other hand, all states enjoy high sea freedoms with respect to navigation, laying of submarine cables, and other lawful uses of the seas, subject to the relevant provisions of UNCLOS.

Coastal states also have jurisdiction over the protection and preservation of the marine environment, marine scientific research, and the establishment and use of artificial islands, installations, and structures in their EEZ.[12] These

---

(Cambridge University Press, Cambridge: 2015); and J. A. Roach, 'Today's Customary Law of the Sea', in *Ocean Development & International Law* (45, 3: 2014) 239–259.

10 See E. Franckx, 'Gaps in Baltic Sea Maritime Boundaries', in H. Ringbom (ed.), *Regulatory Gaps in Baltic Sea Governance – Selected Issues* (Springer: 2018) 7–20.

11 United Nations Convention on the Law of the Sea (adopted 10 December 1982, entered into force 16 November 1994) 1833 UNTS 3, Art. 56(1)(a).

12 UNCLOS, Art. 56(1)(b).

FIGURE 1   Maritime zones in the Baltic Sea

rights are only moderated by specific limitations laid down in UNCLOS or by the general obligation to have due regard for the interests of other states and to observe the general principles, *inter alia*, relating to the protection of the marine environment.

Specific provisions apply to the laying of cables and pipelines. All states are entitled to lay submarine cables and pipelines on the continental shelf of other states, and coastal states may not impede the laying or maintenance of such cables or pipelines "subject to its right to take reasonable measures for the exploration of the continental shelf, the exploitation of its natural resources and the prevention, reduction and control of pollution from pipelines" (UNCLOS Article 79(2)).

Apart from this limitation, which is further detailed in UNCLOS Article 79, the general picture is that coastal states have significant influence over sea-based measures within their EEZ and underlying continental shelf. The rules on 'installations or structures' could be particularly relevant in this context, providing, as they do, the exclusive right for the coastal state to construct, authorize, and regulate the construction, operation, and use of installations and structures in the EEZ and the continental shelf.[13] There is no definition of such installations and structures.

For activities that are not specifically mentioned in UNCLOS Part V on the EEZ, i.e. do not fall within the categories of marine scientific research, resource utilization, environmental protection, etc., the freedoms of the high seas apply. Coastal state authority over such activities is much more limited and mainly subject to the duty of all states to have due regard to the interests of other states.

Closer to the coast, at a maximum distance of 12 nautical miles (nm) from the baseline, the territorial sea forms a part of the coastal state's territory and is hence, as a starting point, subject to the sovereignty of the coastal state.[14] However, the main exception to this is the right of foreign ships to exercise the right of innocent passage in other states' territorial seas. The activities associated with this right are closely linked to navigation and the right would normally not extend to ships involved in sea-based measures. Research or survey activities in foreign states' territorial sea are specifically prohibited under UNCLOS Article 19(2)(j). In other words, coastal states have far-reaching rights to regulate any potentially environmentally harmful or hazardous activities in the vicinity of their coasts, and also have the right to take measures to reduce pollution, such as prohibiting dumping. The sovereignty over the territorial sea also covers the underlying seabed.

In internal waters, i.e. on the landside of the baseline, the law of the sea places no limitations of relevance to sea-based measures. It is accordingly for the coastal state to decide on the usage of these waters in all respects unless it has limited its sovereignty in this regard through treaties or otherwise. National and EU rules accordingly apply in full in this area, unless otherwise specifically provided, while the applicability of the international obligations has to be addressed case-by-case, based on the scope of the conventions concerned.

UNCLOS also contains special provisions regarding enclosed or semi-enclosed seas, providing that the bordering states should cooperate, where appropriate through a regional organization, to implement their rights and

---

13 UNCLOS, Art. 60; and regarding jurisdiction for installations on the continental shelf, see Art. 80.

14 UNCLOS, Arts. 2–4. Exceptions: UNCLOS, Arts. 17–19.

COMBATTING EUTROPHICATION IN THE BALTIC SEA

duties regarding the protection and preservation of the marine environment.[15] Cooperation within the Helsinki Convention framework is obviously of relevance when assessing cooperative arrangements in this regard and HELCOM accordingly plays a potentially significant role in relation to fulfilling the purposes of UNCLOS.

In conclusion, UNCLOS does not offer much guidance with respect to the rights and obligations relating to sea-based measures. It does not foresee these types of activities and even the nature of states' jurisdiction over activities targeting seabed sediments is not entirely clear, as the matter depends, *inter alia*, on the status of the phosphorus tied to the sediment as a 'natural resource' and whether the activity in question is considered to represent 'marine scientific research', 'protection of the marine environment', 'dumping' or involving an 'installation or structure'. Different types of sea-based measures raise somewhat different questions in this regard, as will be discussed in more detail in section 2.6 below.

2.2.1.2   Obligations to Protect and Preserve the Marine Environment

Outside the zonal framework, UNCLOS Part XII includes a number of requirements for states to protect and preserve the marine environment, which apply irrespective of whether or not the activity in question is specifically regulated by UNCLOS and regardless of the maritime zone involved and of the capacity in which the state acts.[16] All states have an obligation to protect the marine environment (Article 192) and must ensure that activities being carried out under their jurisdiction or control do not cause damage by pollution to other states and their environment or do not spread pollution beyond their borders (Article 194(2)). Furthermore, states shall, individually or jointly, take "all measures consistent with this Convention that are necessary to prevent, reduce and control pollution of the marine environment from any source".[17]

'Pollution of the marine environment' is broadly defined to include "the introduction by man of substance or energy into the marine environment", however, the definition also includes a requirement with respect to the (likely) environmental effect of such activity.[18]

---

15   UNCLOS, Part IX, Art. 123. See also Art. 197.
16   UNCLOS, Part XII, Arts. 192–195.
17   UNCLOS, Art. 194(1). Paragraph 3 of the same article goes on to provide that the measures taken shall include measures to "minimize to the fullest possible extent" the release of toxic, harmful and noxious substances, pollution from vessels, and from installations and devices operating in the marine environment.
18   Under UNCLOS Art. 1(4), the full definition of 'pollution of the marine environment' reads "the introduction by man, directly or indirectly, of substances or energy into the marine

Other articles specifically highlight the need for protecting sensitive areas, such as the need to take measures "necessary to protect and preserve rare or fragile ecosystems as well as the habitat of depleted, threatened or endangered species and other forms of marine life",[19] as well as more general duties of cooperation at global and regional levels to prevent, minimize, and control environmental harm.[20] Moreover, when taking such measures to prevent, reduce, or control pollution, states must "act so as not to transfer directly or indirectly damage or hazards from one area to another or transform one type of pollution into another".[21]

UNCLOS was negotiated in the 1970s and early 1980s in the very early days of international environmental law; it, therefore, does not include many of the principles, tools, and approaches that have since been developed and included in later environmental treaties. While UNCLOS includes the fundamental obligation of states not to cause harm to the environment of other states and to prevent pollution from spreading beyond their own jurisdiction,[22] it does not, for example, include references to the precautionary principle, the polluter pays principle, to the use of modern management mechanisms such as the ecosystem approach, or tools such as marine spatial planning.[23]

---

environment, including estuaries, which results or is likely to result in such deleterious effects as harm to living resources and marine life, hazards to human health, hindrance to marine activities, including fishing and other legitimate uses of the sea, impairment of quality for use of sea water and reduction of amenities". The definition is focused on the environmental perspective alone and is not dependent on, e.g. the intention behind the act that caused it. See also P. Birnie, A. Boyle, and C. Redgwell, *International Law and the Environment*, 3rd ed. (Oxford University Press, New York: 2009) 188–189.

19 UNCLOS, Art. 194(5). See also the much less committing Art. 123 on enclosed and semi-enclosed seas, and Art. 197 on regional co-operation.

20 UNCLOS, Art. 197, *et seq.*

21 UNCLOS, Art. 195.

22 UNCLOS, Art. 194(2) reads: "States shall take all measures necessary to ensure that activities under their jurisdiction or control are so conducted as not to cause damage by pollution to other States and their environment, and that pollution arising from incidents or activities under their jurisdiction or control does not spread beyond the areas where they exercise sovereign rights in accordance with this Convention."

23 See also UNCLOS Art. 206 providing for a rather light duty to assess, "as far as practicable", the potential effects of planned activities when they have "reasonable grounds for believing that planned activities under their jurisdiction or control may cause substantial pollution of or significant and harmful changes to the marine environment." This could be seen as a very early variant of an obligation for states to carry out an EIA for activities in their coastal waters.

COMBATTING EUTROPHICATION IN THE BALTIC SEA

However, the subsequent development of such environmental principles cannot be ignored when UNCLOS is applied today.[24] Many key principles have since been developed, not only in terms of substantive content but also in terms of legal status.[25] The 'precautionary principle', in which the lack of scientific certainty shall not be used as a reason to postpone cost-effective measures to prevent environmental degradation, is a case in point. This principle was introduced as Principle 15 in the Rio Declaration in 1992, and has since been reiterated in many international conventions, including the Convention on Biological Diversity (the CBD), the Kyoto Protocol[26] adopted under the UN Framework Convention on Climate Change, the 1995 Fish Stocks Agreement,[27] and the 1996 London Protocol. The principle has also been regarded as representing customary law by international courts.[28]

The environmental obligations and principles of UNCLOS have also been interpreted and developed by international case law. Several international courts and tribunals acting under the UNCLOS umbrella have recently dealt with the status of states' environmental obligations under UNCLOS and concluded, *inter alia*, that states' duty to protect the marine environment encompasses the conservation of the living resources of the sea,[29] and extends

---

24 This is recognized by UNCLOS itself, e.g. when providing that the freedom of the high seas "is exercised under the conditions laid down by this convention and by other rules of international law" (Art. 87(1)).

25 The interpretation of a treaty should, according to Art. 31(3)(c) of the Vienna Convention on the Law of Treaties (adopted 23 May 1969, entered into force 27 January 1980) 1155 UNTS 331 (the Vienna Convention), take into account not only the context but "any relevant rules of international law applicable in the relations between the parties".

26 The 1997 Kyoto Protocol to the United Nations Framework Convention on Climate Change 37 ILM 22(1998).

27 The 1995 United Nations Agreement for the Implementation of the Provisions of the United Nations Convention on the Law of the Sea of 10 December 1982 relating to the Conservation and Management of Straddling Fish Stocks and Highly Migratory Fish Stocks, 2167 UNTS 3.

28 See, e.g. the 2010 decision of the ICJ in *Pulp Mills on the River Uruguay* Case (Argentina v. Uruguay) [2010] ICJ Rep 14, para. 164, and *Responsibilities and Obligations of States Sponsoring Persons and Entities with Respect to Activities in the Area (Advisory Opinion)* [2011] ITLOS Rep 10, para. 135. Yet, even with widespread agreement on the status of the principle as such and its fundamental importance in the environmental decision-making process, there is still plenty of scope for disagreement on the implications of the principle in individual cases. Issues such as whether the identification of a serious risk imposes an obligation to refrain from the activity in question altogether, and questions relating to determining a serious risk and the burden of proof are likely to come up in any concrete dispute.

29 Southern Bluefin Tuna (ITLOS provisional measures, https://www.itlos.org/fileadmin/itlos/documents/cases/case_no_3_4/published/C34-O-27_aug_99.pdf), Para. 70 (accessed

beyond controlling pollution to measures focused primarily on conservation and the preservation of ecosystems[30] and "to the prevention of harms that would affect depleted, threatened, or endangered species indirectly through the destruction of their habitat".[31] Case law, in other words, suggests a development towards a more holistic and integrated understanding of states' environmental obligations than the sectoral regime of UNCLOS might otherwise suggest. The duties in UNCLOS Part XII are to be read as a duty to protect the marine environment as a whole, hence also departing from the needs of the ecosystem.

Of particular relevance for the present context is, finally, also the obligation laid down in Article 204(2) for states to "keep under surveillance the effects of any activities which they permit or in which they engage in order to determine whether these activities are likely to pollute the marine environment."

2.2.2 The London Convention and the London Protocol

The 1972 London Convention and its 1996 Protocol restrict dumping at sea of wastes and other matter that can create hazards to, *inter alia*, marine life.[32] The aim is to protect the marine environment from pollution by dumping. In brief, the London Convention establishes that certain forms of dumping that are listed shall be prohibited and that those that are not prohibited require a permit.[33] The London Protocol goes further, declaring that all dumping shall be prohibited, with the exception of certain wastes that are listed in its Annex 1.[34] However, even the disposal of wastes that are not prohibited, i.e. those listed in Annex 1, require a permit and even then the states are required to consider environmentally preferred alternatives.[35] The Protocol also introduces

---

    2.8.2019); Request for an advisory opinion by Sub-regional fisheries Commission (ITLOS Advisory opinion, https://www.itlos.org/fileadmin/itlos/documents/cases/case_no.21/advisory_opinion_published/2015_21-advop-E.pdf, Para. 120 (accessed 2.8.2019).

30   Chago Islands Marine Protected Area Arbitration (UNCLOS Annex VII Arbitral tribunal, www.pcacases.com/pcadocs/MU-UK%2020150318%20Award.pdf), Para. 538 (accessed 24.1.2019).

31   The Matter of the South China Sea Arbitration (UNCLOS Annex VII Arbitral Tribunal, https://pcacases.com/web/sendAttach/2086), Para. 945 (accessed 2.8.2019).

32   Convention on the Prevention of Marine Pollution by Dumping of Wastes and Other Matter (adopted 29 December 1972, entered into force 30 August 1975) 1046 UNTS 120 (the London Convention); Protocol to the Convention on the Prevention of Marine Pollution by Dumping of Wastes and Other Matter (adopted 7 November 1996, entered into force 24 March 2006) 36 ILM 1 (the London Protocol).

33   London Convention, Art. IV.

34   London Protocol, Art. 4(1)(1).

35   London Protocol, Art. 4(1)(2).

COMBATTING EUTROPHICATION IN THE BALTIC SEA 15

a specific obligation for the states parties to apply a precautionary approach to environmental protection from dumping, which is not mentioned in the Convention.[36]

Dumping is also regulated through UNCLOS, but in less prescriptive terms. UNCLOS only requires that states shall regulate and control pollution by dumping at sea, at least as effectively regulated at sea as provided for in global substantive rules and standards.[37] These obligations are placed not only on the flag state of the ship concerned, but also on coastal states and, more importantly for the present context, on the state where the waste or other matter was loaded.[38]

Both the London Convention and the London Protocol apply to all waters, except to the internal waters of states, hence including both the EEZ and the territorial sea of the states parties. This means that there is little or no room for states to allow any form of dumping in these areas, if not identified as an exception. In addition, the Protocol extends certain parts of its permit procedures to internal waters. The requirements of both instruments also apply to vessels and aircrafts under the flag of the contracting parties, irrespective of their location, and to vessels loading in their territory/territorial sea.[39]

In the Baltic Sea region, as of 29 May 2019 Latvia and Lithuania are the only states that have not ratified either the London Convention or the London Protocol. The Russian Federation and Poland have currently not ratified the Protocol but are parties to the Convention. Denmark, Estonia, Finland, Germany, and Sweden are all parties to both instruments. If sea-based measures are to be taken in cooperation, the different levels of acceptance and ratification of the London Convention and Protocol could affect the possibilities to find a mutual understanding.

The London Convention, like UNCLOS, defines dumping as "deliberate disposal at sea of wastes or other matter from vessels, aircraft, platforms or other man-made structures at sea."[40] However, the Convention also includes some exceptions to this definition. Discharge or waste occurring in the normal operation of ships or other forms of structures at sea are, for example, not included. Nor is deliberate "placement of matter for a purpose other than the

---

36 London Protocol, Art. 3.
37 Article 210(6). To the extent the rules of the London Convention and the Protocol reflect "global rules and standards" under this paragraph, they will accordingly have legal implications even for states that are not parties to these instruments.
38 Article 216 lays down an unqualified obligation for the coastal state, the flag state, and for any state in which the substance is loaded to enforce the rules.
39 London Convention, Arts. 6 and 7; Arts. 7 and 10.
40 London Convention, Art. III(1)(a)(i).

mere disposal thereof" seen as dumping according to the Convention, as long as it does not contravene the aim of the Convention.[41]

The governing bodies of the Convention and the Protocol have established that the scope of the two instruments includes ocean fertilization activities,[42] and have prohibited that activity except for legitimate scientific research. The regulation of ocean fertilization also includes an "Assessment Framework for Scientific Research Involving Ocean Fertilization", which guides parties on how to assess proposals for ocean fertilization research and provides detailed steps for completing an environmental assessment, including risk management and monitoring.[43]

More recently a similar approach has been extended to marine geo-engineering activities more generally. A 2013 amendment of the 1996 Protocol provides that "Contracting Parties shall not allow the placement of matter into the sea from vessels, aircraft, platforms or other man-made structures at sea for marine geoengineering activities listed in Annex 4, unless the listing provides that the activity or the sub-category of an activity may be authorized under a permit."[44] The amendment is not yet in force, but since the new article, along with the related definitions and annexes, represents an interesting example of how novel technological developments with uncertain environmental effects can be accommodated in the existing legal framework, it will be discussed in more detail in section 3.3.3 below.

2.2.3   The Convention on Biological Diversity

The objectives of the Convention on Biological Diversity (CBD) concern the conservation of biological diversity, the sustainable use of its components, and the fair and equitable sharing of the benefits arising out of the utilization of genetic resources.[45] The convention is to be implemented in accordance with the particular conditions of each party and its specific environmental conditions. The parties, which include all Baltic Sea states and the EU, are then to develop national strategies, plans, or programmes for conservation of biological diversity and integrate the conservation and sustainable use of biological

---

41   London Convention, Art. III(1)(b).

42   Resolution LC-LP.1(2008) on the Regulation of Ocean Fertilization, Para. 3, in which 'ocean fertilization' is defined as "any activity undertaken by humans with the principal intention of stimulating primary productivity in the oceans."

43   Resolution LC-LP.2(2010). See also P. Sands and J. Peel, *Principles of International Environmental Law*, 3rd ed. (Cambridge University Press, Cambridge: 2012) 396.

44   New Article 6bis to the 1996 Protocol adopted through Resolution LP4(8).

45   Convention on Biological Diversity (adopted 5 June 1992, entered into force 29 December 1993) 1760 UNTS 79, Art. 1.

COMBATTING EUTROPHICATION IN THE BALTIC SEA

diversity into relevant sectoral plans, programmes, and policies.[46] The provisions of the CBD apply, in relation to each Contracting Party, within the area of its national jurisdiction or beyond the limits of national jurisdiction, in the case of processes and activities, regardless of where their effects occur, carried out under its jurisdiction or control.[47] Hence, sea-based measures undertaken by coastal states in the Baltic Sea will be subject to the rules of the CBD. However, Article 2(2) of the CBD provides that nothing in the convention shall affect rights or obligations under the law of the sea.

Through the work of its Conference of Parties (COP), CBD has shown significant interest in – and support for – the activities in the London Dumping framework aimed at limiting ocean fertilization, *inter alia*, by urging Governments "in accordance with the precautionary approach to ensure that ocean fertilization activities do not take place until there is an adequate scientific basis on which to justify such activities".[48] Similar decisions have also been adopted with respect to other "climate-related geoengineering activities".[49]

2.3 *Regional Rules*
2.3.1 The Helsinki Convention
2.3.1.1 *General*

The Helsinki Convention, being a convention specific to the environmental protection of the Baltic Sea, is of course highly relevant in the present context. It is the only instrument that specifically regulates the marine environment of the Baltic Sea. The Helsinki Convention includes a wide range of activities within its scope. Its commission, HELCOM, has been established as an important platform for monitoring, scientific cooperation, and data-collection, providing important prerequisites for developing more effective approaches to protecting the Baltic Sea environment. The HELCOM framework is, thus, indirectly referred to in the many UNCLOS provisions that refer to further regional environmental collaboration and rule-development through the 'competent international organizations'. Similarly, the Helsinki Convention in itself also represents 'applicable international rules and standards', as far as such references refer to regional marine environmental law-making and enforcement.[50] All coastal states of the Baltic Sea are parties to the Helsinki Convention,

---

46 The CBD, Art. 6.
47 The CBD, Art. 4(b).
48 CBD COP Decision IX/16 C (2008), para. 4.
49 CBD COP Decision X/33 (2010), para. 8 w.
50 UNCLOS, Art. 197 and Section 6 on Enforcement.

which applies to the entire Baltic Sea area, including the internal waters of the parties.[51]

Through the EU's formal participation in the Helsinki Convention, the convention also forms, at least in part, an integral part of EU law. This means that EU member states and EU institutions can rely on the EU's law enforcement apparatus and procedures, which are significantly more powerful than those of general international law that would otherwise apply for implementing the obligations of the Helsinki Convention. Case law from the Court of Justice of the European Union (CJEU or 'the Court') has also confirmed that the EU's participation in an international convention has the effect that the rules of the Convention (which fall under the EU's competence) have precedence over the EU's own directives and regulations.[52] A consequence of this is that if a clear and precise rule of the Helsinki Convention, or its Annexes, conflicts with an EU law, the Helsinki Convention shall prevail. This, however, does not extend to recommendations or other non-binding instruments adopted by HELCOM.

The principal substantive obligation of the Helsinki Convention is that "the Contracting Parties shall individually or jointly take all appropriate legislative, administrative or other relevant measures to prevent and eliminate pollution in order to promote the ecological restoration of the Baltic Sea Area and the preservation of its ecological balance."[53] The Helsinki Convention also requires that the environmental law principles listed in Article 3 are applied for any kind of measures taken.[54] Article 5 contains a requirement to eliminate and prevent pollution of harmful substances from all sources. According to the definition in Article 2(7) and the criteria found in Annex I of the Convention, harmful substances include any substance liable to cause pollution. This shall apply to anthropogenically produced substances liable to cause eutrophication, such as nitrogen and phosphorus compounds. These substances are also found in a priority group of harmful substances in Annex I, i.e. a list of substances that should be given priority by the parties in their implementation of preventive measures.

Besides the requirements found in the Convention's provisions and its annexes, the substantive requirements are usually found in recommendations, which is the main regulatory tool of HELCOM. The Convention has

---

51 Convention on the Protection of the Marine Environment of the Baltic Sea Area (adopted 9 April 1992, entered into force 17 January 2000) 2099 UNTS 195, Art. 1.

52 See, e.g. Case C-344/04 IATA and ELFAA, Para. 35.

53 Helsinki Convention, Art. 3(1).

54 Helsinki Convention, Art. 3(2–6).

also been further developed in its structure and aim with the adoption of the Baltic Sea Action Plan (BSAP) in 2007, which places further emphasis on certain key issues, including eutrophication, and acknowledges the importance of an ecosystem approach. In terms of the ecosystem approach, the BSAP is also operationalizing the HELCOM Vision.[55]

However, from a substantive point of view, the Helsinki Convention, including its annexes, recommendations and action plan, contain little on sea-based measures. Most requirements and approaches taken to combat eutrophication to date have focused on land-based sources and measures to reduce pollution from land. The general approach in the BSAP policy and the related recommendations adopted in recent years have focused on how to encourage states to more effectively and ambitiously implement traditional land-based measures to reduce eutrophication.[56] However, as further discussed in Part 5, the first signs of interest to develop a regulatory framework for sea-based measures have been taken in 2018.

2.3.1.2 Provisions of Relevance for Sea-Based Measures

The Helsinki Convention and the rules and recommendations adopted for its implementation confirm the necessity of significant nutrient pollution reductions in order to achieve the HELCOM Vision of a healthy Baltic Sea and a good environmental status, as required also by EU rules in relation to eutrophication in the Baltic Sea. However, neither the Helsinki Convention, the BSAP, nor the EU Marine Strategy Framework Directive (MSFD)[57] regulate how these reductions are to be achieved.

The Helsinki Convention regulates dumping and also includes certain requirements on EIAs, but apart from that, does not directly address matters of relevance for sea-based measures. Even if the convention is generally broad

---

55 "The aim is to reach HELCOM's vision for good environmental status in the Baltic Sea", BSAP Eutrophication segment, 7; The BSAP Preamble, 4. See also: "HELCOM Ecological Objectives for an Ecosystem Approach", document for HELCOM Stakeholder Conference on the Baltic Sea Action Plan, Helsinki, Finland, 7 March 2006, 1f, where HELCOM declares the connections between EU legislation, the CBD, the HELCOM Vision, its Ecological Objectives and the BSAP and furthermore states that the BSAP is the tool of implementation of an ecosystem approach.

56 See, e.g. the HELCOM Copenhagen Ministerial Declaration, "Taking Further Action to Implement the Baltic Sea Action Plan – Reaching Good Environmental Status for a healthy Baltic Sea", Copenhagen Denmark, 3 October 2013, including the acts adopted, HELCOM Palette of optional agro-environmental measures and Recommendations.

57 Directive 2008/56/EC of the European Parliament and of the Council of 17 June 2008 establishing a framework for community action in the field of marine environmental policy (Marine Strategy Framework Directive) OJ L 164/19.

and cross-sectoral in scope, it includes no provisions on dredging, or on structures or installations that would be required for oxygen pumping. Instead, the main structure and tenet of the Convention is a general approach towards any kind of pollution and any measures taken in the region to reduce eutrophication. In other words, the Helsinki Convention, too, governs sea-based measures by means of general environmental principles. In many respects, however, these principles are more elaborate at a regional level than those included in UNCLOS.

The Helsinki Convention requires its parties to "take all appropriate legislative, administrative or other relevant measures to prevent and eliminate pollution in order to promote the ecological restoration of the Baltic Sea Area and the preservation of its ecological balance."[58] It also applies the precautionary principle, by obliging the parties to:

> take preventive measures when there is reason to assume that substances or energy introduced, directly or indirectly, into the marine environment may create hazards to human health, harm living resources and marine ecosystems, damage amenities or interfere with other legitimate uses of the sea even when there is no conclusive evidence of a causal relationship between inputs and their alleged effects.[59]

Both principles refer to the ecosystem, as does the obligation in Article 15 for the parties to "take all appropriate measures with respect to the Baltic Sea Area and its coastal ecosystems influenced by the Baltic Sea to conserve natural habitats and biological diversity and to protect ecological processes."[60] With the adoption of the BSAP, the HELCOM regime further acknowledged and operationalized the ecosystem approach. Even if generic and difficult to operationalize in the abstract, these principles may be of importance when balancing the interests involved in sea-based measures.

The Convention also reiterates the obligations of the Espoo Convention on establishing an EIA and notifying other states concerned[61] and includes regulation regarding the exploration and exploitation of the seabed and its subsoil.[62]

---

58   Helsinki Convention, Art. 3(1).
59   Helsinki Convention, Art. 3(2).
60   Helsinki Convention, Art. 15.
61   Helsinki Convention, Art. 7. On the Espoo Convention, see further below, in section 2.4.1.
62   Helsinki Convention, Arts. 11 and 12.

COMBATTING EUTROPHICATION IN THE BALTIC SEA 21

More importantly, for present purposes, the Helsinki Convention prohibits dumping, with the main exemption only for dredged material, but even in the case of dumping of such materials, strict requirements on permits and other precautions are set out in Annex v.[63] Dumping of dredged materials must be carried out under a prior special permit issued by the appropriate national authority, and only then within the area of the internal waters and the territorial sea of the contracting party. If a party wants to dump such materials outside its internal waters and territorial sea it requires prior consultation with HELCOM.[64] For this purpose, HELCOM has recently adopted specific guidelines regarding dumping of dredged materials and the processes or requirements that states parties shall apply.[65]

The Helsinki Convention, in other words, provides a general ban on dumping and hence goes beyond the rules of the London Convention to which many of the Baltic coastal states are still parties. Moreover, since the Helsinki Convention, as opposed to the global dumping rules, has a geographical scope which includes internal waters, the Baltic Sea states do not have the option to apply lighter national rules in these areas.[66]

As the purpose of dredging in the context of sea-based measures is to remove the sediment without returning the dredged materials to the sea, the provisions on dredging do not find application here. It may be worth mentioning, however, that the effects of dredging can in some respects be compared to dumping of such materials, e.g. as regards the turbidity it causes. On this basis, it has been suggested that if dumping of dredged materials is restricted, the dredging activity itself should also be undertaken with corresponding precaution and restrictions.[67]

Finally, the Helsinki Convention places obligations on states to take all appropriate measures to "conserve natural habitats and biological diversity and to protect ecological processes",[68] and includes a variety of cooperative obligations, which will be of relevance for assessing the manner in which sea-based measures will be undertaken.

---

63   Helsinki Convention, Art. 11.
64   Helsinki Convention, Annex v, Regulation 1(b).
65   HELCOM Guidelines for Management of Dredged Material at Sea, adopted by HELCOM 36-2015 on 4 March 2015.
66   Helsinki Convention, Art. 1.
67   Swedish Environmental Protection Agency (Naturvårdsverket), Report, "*Muddring och hantering av muddermassor: Vägledning om tillämpning av 11 och 15 kap Miljöbalken*", Miljörättsavdelningen 2010-02-18, 34ff. [in Swedish].
68   Helsinki Convention, Art. 15.

2.3.2 EU Laws for Water and Marine Environment
2.3.2.1 *General*

There are several different kinds of EU laws that are relevant for a general approach to combating eutrophication. One set of EU laws regulate activities related to land-based measures and sectors and thus falls beyond the scope here. Another category of EU laws, which will be addressed here, consists of instruments that have a more general and process-oriented focus, based on the ecosystem approach, focusing specifically on water and the marine environment. The main legislative instruments of this kind are Marine Strategy Framework Directive (MSFD), Directive 2000/60/EC on establishing a framework for Community action in the field of water policy (Water Framework Directive, WFD), and Directive 2014/89/EU on establishing a framework for maritime spatial planning (Maritime Spatial Planning Directive, MSPD), which will be further presented in sections 2.3.2.2 and 2.3.2.3 below.

Moreover, certain EU environmental rules of more horizontal applicability will be of relevance for sea-based measures. The EIA and Waste Framework Directives are discussed in sections 2.4.2 and 2.3.3.2, while the directives aimed at protecting biodiversity and nature, i.e. the Habitats and Birds Directives, are briefly reviewed in section 2.3.3.1.

The EU rules that specifically relate to the marine environment normally clarify their geographical scope.[69] Hence, it is clear that the MSPD and the MSFD primarily apply to marine waters, defined as waters, the seabed, and subsoil on the seaward side of the territorial sea baseline extending to the outmost reach of the area where a member state has and/or exercises jurisdictional rights in accordance with the UNCLOS (i.e. up to 200 nm from the baseline).[70] The WFD applies to inland surface waters, transitional waters, coastal waters, and groundwater.[71] Coastal waters, according to the WFD, is the surface waters on the landward side of a line 1 nm on the seaward side from

---

69　More generally, the geographical extent of EU rules has been subject to some uncertainty. At least with respect to certain instruments, the Court has confirmed that EU law applies to activities falling within the coastal member state's jurisdiction or sovereign right to the extent that the state has exercised its sovereign rights. See e.g. Cases C-6/2004 and C-111/05. The Waste Framework Directive is not clear on this point, while the EIA Directive extends to projects affecting directly or indirectly 'water' without further specification.

70　MSFD, Art. 3(1)(a) and (b).

71　Directive 2000/60/EC of the European Parliament and of the Council of 23 October 2000 establishing a framework for Community action in the field of water policy (Water Framework Directive) OJ L 327/1 (the WFD), Arts. 1 and 2. Art. 2(6) defines 'transitional waters' as "bodies of surface water in the vicinity of river mouths which are partly saline in character as a result of their proximity to coastal waters but which are substantially influenced by freshwater flows."

the baseline.[72] The geographical scope of the MSFD and the WFD hence overlap, but the MSFD then only applies to coastal waters in so far as particular aspects of the environmental status of the marine environment are not already addressed through the WFD.[73]

2.3.2.2 The EU Marine Strategy Framework Directive and the Water Framework Directive

The MSFD and the WFD are complementary in scope and will be presented together here. The MSFD is the main legal act at EU level for addressing the environment of the Baltic Sea. The aim of the MSFD is for the states to adopt a marine strategy with a 'Programme of Measures' with the goal to achieve "good environmental status".[74] The goal of good environmental status seen in relation to eutrophication means that "human-induced eutrophication is minimised, especially adverse effects thereof, such as losses in biodiversity, ecosystem degradation, harmful algae blooms and oxygen deficiency in bottom waters."[75]

The provisions in the MSFD include a requirement to restore marine ecosystems where they have been adversely affected.[76] The latter could include taking, *inter alia*, sea-based measures. The WFD, similar to the MSFD, adopts a general goal-oriented approach with the aim to achieve good status through adopting 'River Basin Management Plans' with 'Programmes of Measures'.[77] In order to operationalize the goal of good status in the WFD, however, member states are also to define the ecological objectives for each type of water. In order to achieve those ecological objectives, states are also obliged to take further supplementary measures in order to provide for the improvement of the waters covered by the Directive.

Both directives include a rule aimed at preventing environmental deterioration.[78] The CJEU has interpreted this rule strictly in its case law on the WFD, by ruling that any activity – in that case, the activity concerned was dredging – that will lead to deterioration, even on a temporary basis, shall be prohibited in accordance with the non-deterioration rule.[79] This interpretation of the WFD significantly limits the scope for EU member states to approve sea-based

---

72 WFD, Art. 2(7).

73 MSFD, Art. 3(1)(b).

74 MSFD, Arts. 5(2)(b) and 13.

75 MSFD, Arts. 13(1), 9(1) and Annex I.

76 MSFD, Art. 1(2)(b).

77 WFD, Arts. 1 and 11.

78 MSFD, Art. 1(2)(a) and WFD Art. 4.

79 Case C-461/13 Bund v Germany (the *Weser* case). See section 2.3.4.2 below.

measures to abate eutrophication in the internal and coastal waters (up to 1 nm from the baseline). While it is not certain that a similar interpretation would apply to the MSFD,[80] the ruling must be considered by authorities when making the choice of method or technology of sea-based measures, in view of the scientific uncertainties that are involved. Both the WFD and the MSFD also emphasize international law and the contribution to the enforcement of international agreements applicable to the subject matter. The international rules and principles discussed above will accordingly also have an impact on how EU law is applied and understood.

2.3.2.3 *The Marine Spatial Planning Directive*

The MSPD creates a platform for the EU member states to make better planning for the use of maritime areas and the marine waters, taking into account the land-sea interface and interaction.[81] Maritime spatial planning aims at planning the uses of the sea, alongside other substantial or procedural limitations that may apply, such as nature conservation sites, etc.

Under the MSPD, the member states shall set up maritime spatial plans that identify the spatial and temporal distribution of relevant existing and future activities and uses in their marine waters.[82] The plans will provide guidance for the usage of the different marine areas. Even if the plans are non-binding, they will matter in relation to sea-based measures since the activities included in the plans should be given priority if other uses would conflict with the designated activities. However, the MSPD only applies to the marine waters of member states. It does not, therefore, apply to coastal waters or parts thereof falling under a member state's town and country planning, provided that this is communicated in its maritime spatial plans.[83] Hence, for sea-based measures being pursued in the coastal areas or in the internal waters, which seems to be the case for the majority of prospective measures foreseen today, the national planning regulation will be more important.[84] The actual balancing and decisions in relation to planning will be made in the plans themselves, i.e. by national authorities.

---

80   See section 2.3.4.3 below.

81   MSPD, Art. 4.

82   MSPD, Art. 8(1).

83   MSPD, Art. 2(1). Marine and coastal waters are defined by reference to the definitions in the MSFD and WFD.

84   For the Swedish situation, see also Havs- och vattenmyndighetens (SwAM) rapport 2015:2, *Havsplanering – nuläge 2014: Statlig planering i territorialhav och ekonomisk zon*, Diarienummer 137-2014, February 2015, 44ff. [in Swedish].

COMBATTING EUTROPHICATION IN THE BALTIC SEA

2.3.3 Other EU Instruments

2.3.3.1 *The Habitats Directive and the Birds Directive*

The Habitats and Birds Directives primarily aim to protect important habitats and species.[85] The purpose of these directives is to ensure biodiversity through the conservation of natural habitats, including of species protected in either the Habitats Directive or in the Birds Directive – so-called Natura 2000 sights.[86] This aim is regulated both through specific protection of different species as well as through requirements on the protection of habitats.[87]

The protection of these species and habitats is operationalized through preventing activities that could have significant adverse effects on protected species and habitats in these areas. The Natura 2000 habitats create a European ecological network of special areas of conservation.[88] The Habitats Directive, thus, requires that, in such areas, member states take appropriate steps to avoid the deterioration of natural habitats and the habitats of species, as well as the disturbance of the species for which the areas have been designated. This is in so far as such disturbance could be significant in relation to the objectives of the Directive.[89]

In such areas, a plan or project can only be permitted after it is ascertained that it will not adversely affect the integrity of the site concerned. This is required regardless of whether the project is planned to take place in the area or outside.[90] A similar provision exists in the CBD. The Habitats Directive is applicable across the EU territory, i.e. in the territory of the member states and the EEZ, and particularly in relation to those habitats and specially protected areas designated by a member state.[91] If a member state, in other words, has designated an area for habitat protection, it will significantly restrict the use of the area and its surrounding, including the extent to which sea-based measures can be undertaken.[92]

---

85 Directive 2009/147/EC of the European Parliament and of the Council of 30 November 2009 on the conservation of wild birds (the Birds Directive) OJ L 20/7, Arts. 1 and 2; Council Directive 92/43/EEC of 21 May 1992 on the conservation of natural habitats and of wild fauna and flora (the Habitats Directive) OJ L 206/7, Art. 2.

86 Habitats Directive, Arts. 2 and 3.

87 Birds Directive, Arts. 1–4; Habitats Directive, Arts. 2–4.

88 Habitats Directive, Art. 3(1).

89 Habitats Directive, Art. 6(2).

90 Habitats Directive, Art. 6(3).

91 Habitats Directive, Art. 2.

92 Swedish Environmental Protection Agency (Naturvårdsverket), Report, *Muddring och hantering av muddermassor: Vägledning om tillämpning av 11 och 15 kap Miljöbalken*, Miljörättsavdelningen 2010-02-18, 34ff. [in Swedish].

The specific protection of species is relevant in this context to the extent that sea-based measures could pose a threat to a specific marine species, and this would limit the possibilities to take measures in relation to the directives. The protection of habitats at sea could similarly have an effect on the location of sea-based measures since projects in or nearby a protected area are only permitted if it is certain that they will not adversely affect the area or its species.

On the other hand, another perspective is that sea-based measures could be encouraged if they are likely to enhance the marine environment in the protected area or create better conditions for a protected species in the long run.

2.3.3.2 The Waste Framework Directive

The Waste Framework Directive lays down measures to protect the environment and human health by preventing or reducing the adverse impacts of the generation and management of waste, and by reducing the overall impact of resource use and improving the efficiency of such use.[93] It sets out the basic concepts and definitions related to waste management, such as definitions of waste, recycling, and recovery. The aim and main requirement of the Directive is that waste shall be managed without endangering human health and harming the environment, and it is based on, *inter alia*, the polluter pays principle.[94] It also clarifies the criteria for when waste ceases to be waste and on how to distinguish between waste and by-products.[95] While this Directive is not directly applicable to marine activities and will mainly have impact through its implementation by the member states, it is still important to understand its basic principles and its potential significance for the operation of sea-based measures. This is because it will, for example, set the framework for how to handle dredged materials and play an important role in the definition and potential recycling of such phosphorus-rich materials. An interesting and important thing to note in this regard is the specific restriction of its application, stating that sediments being relocated inside surface water for different purposes are only excluded from the scope of the Directive as long as they are proven non-hazardous.[96]

---

93   Directive 2008/98/EC of the European Parliament and of the Council of 19 November 2008 on waste and repealing certain Directives (Waste Framework Directive) OJ L 312/3, Art. 1.
94   Waste Framework Directive, Arts. 13 and 14.
95   Waste Framework Directive, Arts. 5 and 6.
96   Waste Framework Directive, Art. 2(3).

COMBATTING EUTROPHICATION IN THE BALTIC SEA 27

2.3.4   Assessment

2.3.4.1   *The Role of the Marine Directives*

Through the two marine framework directives, EU law, directly and indirectly, addresses every kind of marine activity which may entail the reduction of water quality. The WFD involves the most direct limitations in this regard. It is directly relevant for dredging activities, but in view of its focus on any activity that could involve environmental degradation, it could also be applied to the chemical treatment of the seabed or oxygen pumping.

The WFD applies to internal waters, including inland surface waters, transitional waters, coastal waters, and groundwater, and has a geographical scope which stretches, in total, a maximum of 1 nm beyond the baseline on the seaward side. The exception lies in respect of chemical status for which it shall include territorial sea and may hence extend up to 12 nm from the baseline.[97] In comparison, the MSFD is applicable to marine waters from the baseline on the seaward side extending to the outmost reach of the area where a member state has and/or exercises jurisdictional rights in accordance with UNCLOS.[98] To the extent the two directives overlap (for waters within the 1 nm limit from the baseline), the MSFD gives precedence to the WFD by only including "coastal waters as defined by Directive 2000/60/EC, their seabed and their subsoil, in so far as particular aspects of the environmental status of the marine environment are not already addressed through that Directive or other Community legislation."[99]

If the WFD is applicable, i.e. if the measure is taken in internal waters or less than 1 nm from the baseline, the environmental objectives of the WFD become central to permitting the activities. The general aim of the WFD is to create a framework for the protection of water for a number of different purposes. This includes preventing further deterioration and to enhance the status of aquatic ecosystems, with regard to their water needs, terrestrial ecosystems, and wetlands directly depending on the aquatic ecosystems.[100] The framework set out for this protection is based on environmental objectives and the general aim to reach good ecological/chemical water status. In order to assess the ecological status, member states are to identify river basin districts and make river basin management plans. In order to be able to monitor the environmental status of these river basins, the member states are first to undertake an initial assessment of the water status in each river basin, as a means to classify the

---

97   WFD, Arts. 1 and 2.
98   MSFD, Art. 3(1)a.
99   MSFD, Art. 3(1)(b).
100   WFD, Art. 1.

water status from which to track the development towards better water quality. The protective framework also prohibits the deterioration of water quality for any of the waters assessed and classified, based on the principle of no deterioration.[101]

The classification of water status is based on a range of quality elements or indicators, adjusted to the specific types and characteristics of waters and the particular environmental objectives. Depending on these quality indicators, waters are classified as having high, good, moderate, poor, and bad status. The sum of the level or existence of all quality elements – as specifically described in the Annexes to the Directive – decides the general quality level or the general status classification. A water body is classified in the class immediately below as soon as the ratio of one of the quality elements falls below the level for the current class, according to the principle "one out all out". This is linked to the definition of "surface water status" in Article 2 of the WFD: the status is to be determined by the poorer of the ecological status and the chemical status of the body of surface water.[102] This classification and the environmental objectives are factors that become central when assessing whether the activities connected to sea-based measures could be permitted since they could potentially harm the quality elements and the ecological status.

Since the WFD is a directive, these rules are to be implemented through national law.[103] It is therefore up to individual member state legislation to specify how different areas are assessed, classified, and monitored. As is discussed in more detail Part 4 below, in Finland, implementation is ensured through the Water Resource Management Act, while in Sweden, the directive is primarily implemented through Chapter 5 of the Environmental Code and the Water Management Ordinance. Further specification and harmonization of the national requirements may be achieved not only by means of amendments to the WFD[104] but also through judgments and rulings by the CJEU. A particularly relevant ruling on the interpretation and application of the WFD rules is the *Weser* judgment from 2015. Since this case has wide consequences for

---

101   WFD, Art. 4.

102   WFD, Art. 2(17); Case C-461/13 Bund v Germany (the *Weser* case), Para. 59.

103   Under the Treaty on the Functioning of the European Union, Art. 288, directives do not have direct applicability. However, case law by the CJEU has confirmed the "vertical" direct effect of directives, which permits citizens to invoke the non-implementation of the directive against a member state (but not against private persons) in case national implementation does not meet the requirements of the directive once the deadline for implementation has expired.

104   WFD has been amended seven times since it was adopted in 2000.

COMBATTING EUTROPHICATION IN THE BALTIC SEA   29

activities affecting the water status in an area covered by the WFD, it deserves more detailed scrutiny here.

2.3.4.2   *The* Weser *Case*

The *Weser* case[105] was initiated by a permit procedure for a project that included dredging activities in the river Weser in Germany. In court proceedings concerning a potential permit for a planned project, the German Federal Administrative Court ("Bundesverwaltungsgericht") asked the Court of Justice of the European Union (CJEU or "the Court") for a preliminary ruling on the interpretation of the extension of the WFD ecological objectives and the non-deterioration principle.

The case in the Court focused particularly on the obligation of member states to achieve 'good surface water status' provided under Article 4(1)(a)(ii) of the WFD, a goal that all bodies of water in the EU territories ought to have achieved by 2015.[106] The most central question was whether the member states are required to refuse authorisation for a project where it may cause the deterioration of, *inter alia*, the status of a water body, or where it jeopardizes the attainment of good surface water status in accordance with the general requirements laid down by the Directive.[107]

The questions were divided into two main themes. The first theme concerned the legal status of the quality standards set out by the WFD: Are they only goals for management planning or are they binding for concrete authorizations of projects and permit decisions? The second theme concerned the way the standards were to be applied and focused more specifically on how the term "no deterioration" should be understood.[108]

The Court ruled that the objectives of the WFD are legally binding and involve obligations for member states even with respect to individual project approvals.[109] The member states are, accordingly, obliged to refuse authorisation of individual projects estimated to compromise the objectives. The Court also took a strong stance on the so-called non-deterioration principle, which

---

105   Case C-461/13 Bund v Germany (the *Weser* case).

106   T. Paloniitty, 'Analysis: The Weser Case: Case C-461/13 BUND V GERMANY', in *Journal of Environmental Law* (vol. 28, no. 1: 2016) 151–158, doi: 10.1093/jel/eqvo32.

107   Case C-461/13 Bund v Germany, para. 29.

108   H. F. M. W. van Rijswick and C. W. Backes, 'Ground Breaking Landmark Case on Environmental Quality Standards?: The Consequences of the CJEU "*Weser*-judgment" (C-461/13) for Water Policy and Law and Quality Standards in EU Environmental Law', in *Journal for European Environmental & Planning Law* (vol. 12: 2015) 363–377, at 368.

109   Case C-461/13 Bund v Germany, paras. 31–32.

was regarded as binding the member states to the extent that no decline of the quality of the surface waters is allowed.

Importantly, for present purposes, the Court also dealt with the questions as to whether the wider intentions of a project would have any impact in the assessment, i.e. whether a more long-term goal of better environmental status would somehow be able to compensate for a potential short-term deterioration of the ecological status. The Court found that "deterioration of the status" of a body of surface water covers deterioration which does not result in any other classification of the water body. This means that it suffices for only one quality element to deteriorate in order for it to violate the non-deterioration principle of the Directive.[110] Through a textual interpretation of the WFD, the Court concluded that the balancing between long-term and short-term consequences in relation to activities that deteriorate the ecological surface status should only be undertaken through the derogations foreseen in Article 4(7) of the Directive.[111]

In summary, the judgment means that member states are required to refuse authorization for an individual project where it may cause a deterioration of, *inter alia*, the status of a body of surface water or where it jeopardizes the attainment of good surface water status, unless the exemption procedures of Article 4(7) are applied.

In the case of sea-based measures, the relevant interests are, on the one hand, the attainment or maintenance of the Directive's water status objectives and the fulfilment of the non-deterioration principle and, on the other hand, the significance of an undertaking requiring derogation. According to the reasoning of the Court in *Weser*, it seems that impairment of the quality of the water body could be justified through derogations where the interests favouring a project are sufficiently significant.[112] However, derogations can only be granted under certain specific circumstances.

Moreover, even for the derogations found in Article 4(7), the WFD still requires that "all practicable steps are taken to mitigate the adverse impact on the status of the body of water", that "the reasons for those modifications or alterations are of overriding public interest and/or the benefits to the environment

---

110   Case C-461/13 Bund v Germany, para. 55.

111   Case C-461/13 Bund v Germany, Para. 68. See also T. Paloniitty, 2016, 157; Common Implementation Strategy for the Water Framework Directive and the Floods Directive, Guidance Doc no 36, *Exemptions to the Environmental Objectives according to Art. 4(7): New modifications to the physical characteristics of surface water bodies, alterations to the level of groundwater, or new sustainable human development activities* – Document endorsed by EU Water Directors at their meeting in Tallinn on 4–5 December 2017.

112   Paloniitty, 2016, 157.

COMBATTING EUTROPHICATION IN THE BALTIC SEA

and to society of achieving the objectives ... are outweighed by the benefits of the new modifications or alterations to human health, to the maintenance of human safety or to sustainable development", and that "the beneficial objectives served by those modifications or alterations of the water body cannot for reasons of technical feasibility or disproportionate cost be achieved by other means, which are a significantly better environmental option."

The application of derogations according to Article 4(7) has also been reviewed by the Court. In the *Schwarze Sulm case*,[113] the Court clarified the possibilities of states to allow projects despite their negative impact on the water environment. The Court confirmed that member states must be allowed a certain margin of discretion when assessing a specific project under the exemptions in Article 4(7), as long as all conditions set out are carefully examined in forming the basis of the decision, including measures to mitigate the negative impact.[114] The paragraph requires, *inter alia*, that "all practicable steps are taken to mitigate the adverse impact" (sub-para. (a)), that any modification or alteration of water quality is foreseen in the river basin management plan (sub-para. (b)) and, in particular, that "the beneficial objectives served by those modifications or alterations of the water body cannot for reasons of technical feasibility or disproportionate cost be achieved by other means, which are a significantly better environmental option." (sub-para. (d)).

According to the judgment, member states do retain the possibility to balance adverse effects with mitigation matters, or perhaps to justify an impairment or deterioration of the water status with potential long-term positive effects for its environmental status, if it is assumed that the measures are successful.[115] Still, it is a moot point how the assessment of these conditions would play out for sea-based measures, given that they are not yet well established and in view of the uncertainty of their short-term and long-term effects. It is also unclear how they should be compared to land-based measures with a slow but widely acknowledged impact.

2.3.4.3   *The Application of the* Weser *Case to Marine Strategy Framework Directive*

Another important question related to the *Weser* case is whether an analogy can be made to the application of the MSFD. Like the WFD, the MSFD includes

---

113   Case C-346/14 Commission v Republic of Austria (*Schwarze Sulm*).

114   Case C-346/14 Commission v Republic of Austria, paras. 74, and 80–81.

115   See also J. Söderasp, *Law in Integrated and Adaptive Governance of Freshwaters: A Study of the Swedish Implementation of the EU Water Framework Directive*, Doctoral Thesis (Luleå University of Technology, Luleå: 2018), 66f; van Rijswick and Backes, 2015, 16.

a non-deterioration rule, which could suggest that the interpretations made in the *Weser* ruling could be applied analogously. However, many aspects of the assessment of indicators, environmental status, and the programs of measures in the MSFD are designed rather differently from the approach in the WFD. While the general principles of the *Weser* ruling could maybe be seen as parallel in relation to the aim and application of MSFD, the general conclusions are probably not directly transferable. One important difference is that the areas protected by the MSFD are much larger than in the WFD, and are hence also more difficult to monitor and control.[116] For such reasons, it is generally not possible to connect one specific plan, project, or other sources of pollution to a specific occurrence of deterioration under the MSFD. The more general purpose and approach of the MSFD is to steer the general legislation and application of laws in a direction towards pollution reduction. Hence, in contrast to the WFD, the MSFD does not seek to establish limits to specific projects but rather acts as a general adaptive instrument based on a more general approach.

To the extent that parallels can be made, though, the *Weser* ruling makes it clear that adaptive and flexible legislation, based on ecosystem indicators, is not just a general instrument of guidance to be used as a planning tool. These instruments set out concrete requirements for the states to implement and follow at every level. Hence, it follows that also the requirements of the MSFD are to be acknowledged as binding and should be implemented strictly, otherwise the Court could interfere. It seems clear, for example, that any project, permit, or other activity that would clearly contradict with the goal of the MSFD and the ecological indicators used for assessing the process towards the goal would represent a violation of the MSFD. Yet, as was concluded above, the assessment on what a strict implementation entails in practice will probably have to be handled differently for the MSFD in comparison to the WFD, simply due to the different scope and degree of specificity of the two instruments.

2.4 Environmental Impact Assessments

2.4.1 The Espoo Convention

The EIA procedure is an important instrument for reviewing and mapping the knowledge of the direct and indirect effects of the planned project or activity, and potential precautionary measures that are specific to any activity or measures that have potentially hazardous effects on the environment. More specific procedural requirements are found both at EU level (the EIA Directive) and at

---

116   Under Art. 4(2) of the MSFD, member states may further divide the marine regions into marine sub-regions. However, even the marine sub-regions adopted hereunder are considerably larger than the water bodies referred to in the WFD.

COMBATTING EUTROPHICATION IN THE BALTIC SEA 33

international level (the Espoo Convention). Moreover, national implementing laws may include additional requirements of what should be included in an EIA, and what activities should be reviewed on the basis of EIAS.

The Espoo Convention aims for states to take early action to avert danger by notifying and consulting with neighboring states on major projects that are under consideration and that could have an impact on the environment beyond national borders.[117] To this end, the Espoo Convention specifically lists certain activities that should always fall under this obligation.[118] None of these are directly applicable to sea-based measures, but the Convention also contains a possibility for activating the EIA rules in relation to other activities which are considered likely to cause a significant adverse transboundary impact.[119] This could be applied to the suggested sea-based measures. The EIA Directive includes similar obligations, but with a more narrow range of targeted activities which do not seem to cover sea-based measures.

The Espoo Convention potentially applies to sea-based measures since such measures, regardless of where in the Baltic Sea they are applied, may entail transboundary environmental impacts. The main obligation found in the Espoo Convention is for states to "prevent, reduce and control significant adverse transboundary environmental impact from proposed activities."[120]

Among the key requirements is to adopt an EIA and to consult with neighboring states according to the Espoo Convention. Since potential environmental threats are not limited to the state that determines a certain activity, the Espoo Convention requires that states take early action to avert danger by notifying and consulting with neighboring states on major projects that are under consideration, which could have an impact on the environment beyond national borders.[121] To this end, the Espoo Convention specifically lists certain activities that are always considered "likely to cause a significant adverse transboundary impact".[122] This list includes, *inter alia*, "waste-disposal installations for the incineration, chemical treatment or landfill of toxic and dangerous wastes",[123] but not dredging or other specifically marine activities.

---

117 Convention on Environmental Impact Assessment in a Transboundary Context (adopted 25 February 1991, entered into force 10 September 1997) 1989 UNTS 309 (the Espoo Convention) Art. 2.
118 Espoo Convention, Art. 2(2) and Appendix I.
119 Espoo Convention, Art. 2(5).
120 Espoo Convention, Art. 2(1).
121 Espoo Convention, Art. 2.
122 Espoo Convention, Art. 2(2) and Appendix I.
123 Espoo Convention, Appendix I (10).

The EIA rules may also be activated in relation to activities other than those listed if they are likely to cause a significant adverse transboundary impact.[124] This option could be applicable in relation to sea-based measures, to the extent any such (likely) impact could extend beyond national borders.

Russia is the only Baltic Sea coastal state that is not a party to the Espoo Convention, but consultation and EIA is required by all other coastal states, also on the basis of the EU Directive on EIAS (discussed in the next section), and must at least be taken into consideration when studying the consequences and effects of the measures planned. There is also a parallel requirement in the Helsinki Convention providing that the parties should communicate their EIA when it is likely that an activity could cause significant adverse effects to the environment.[125] This obligation is only applicable to states that are subject to such requirements under other laws, such as the Espoo Convention, and does not thus create any direct obligation for Russia. However, establishing an EIA and notifying the states concerned has been considered to represent a general principle of international environmental law under certain circumstances, hence placing limitations even for non-parties such as Russia.[126]

Based on such criteria, sea-based measures must be assessed in relation to where and at what scale they are undertaken. Measures in a closed bay or close to the coast seem less likely to have transboundary effects, despite the sensitivity of the sea. Conversely, if large-scale sea-based measures were to be undertaken in open waters, perhaps in one of the deep-sea basins of the Baltic Sea, measures are very likely to meet the criteria for triggering the requirements under the Espoo Convention.

The requirement to undertake EIAS is only a procedural requirement that does not as such control or restrict the measures taken. However, EIAS are relevant in this context since it is through this process that the different potential risks, benefits, and other interest or issues are to be presented and assessed. This information, and any knowledge gaps it may highlight may be of critical importance when applying the (separate) national permit procedures, discussed in section 4.2, to which the EIA shall be submitted.

---

124   Espoo Convention, Art. 2(5).
125   Helsinki Convention, Art. 7.
126   The ICJ Judgments in the Case Concerning *Pulp Mills on the River Uruguay* (Argentina v. Uruguay), judgment of 20 April, 2010, and cases involving Nicaragua and Costa Rica, judgment of 16 December 2015 (paras. 104 and 146–162), recognize that carrying out an EIA is a duty under international law.

2.4.2 The EIA Directive

The EIA Directive is not specifically connected to marine activities or the protection of the marine environment. It mainly requires that member states shall adopt measures to ensure that any project that is "likely to have significant effects on the environment"[127] is reviewed and made subject to a requirement for development consent.[128] This procedure should also include an EIA.[129] A 'project' is defined as "the execution of construction works or of other installations or schemes" or "other interventions in the natural surroundings and landscape including those involving the extraction of mineral resources."[130] Thus, it could apply to sea-based measures, even though the extent to which impacts must be assessed varies individually in relation to the specific activities. The Directive requires that member states adopt all measures necessary to ensure that, before development consent is given, projects likely to have significant effects on the environment by virtue, *inter alia*, of their nature, size, or location are made subject to a requirement for development consent and an assessment with regard to their effects on the environment.[131]

The Directive specifically lists types of projects that fall within the requirements.[132] It does not apply to projects that are adopted by a specific act of national legislation because, according to the objectives of the Directive, it is then seen as being achieved through the legislative process.[133]

The EIA Directive is also connected to the Espoo Convention and imposes a similar communication obligation on member states. If a member state is aware that a project is likely to have significant effects on the environment in another member state, it must inform the state concerned and provide, *inter alia*, a description of the project so that the state concerned can enter into consultations about the project.[134]

The Directive also outlines a number of criteria for projects that are subject to the different procedures, as well as more specific requirements on the reports, assessments, and processes. Article 4 provides that for certain projects, listed in the Directive's Annex I, it is mandatory to follow the procedures and

---

127 Directive 2011/92/EU of the European Parliament and of the Council of 13 December 2011 on the assessment of the effects of certain public and private projects on the environment (EIA Directive) OJ L 26/1, Art. 1(1).
128 EIA Directive, Art. 2(1).
129 EIA Directive, Art. 2(2).
130 EIA Directive, Art. 1(2)(a).
131 EIA Directive, Art. 2(1).
132 EIA Directive, Art. 4 and Annexes I and II.
133 EIA Directive, Art. 1 and 2; see also D. Langlet and S. Mahmoudi, *EU Environmental Law and Policy* (Oxford University Press, Oxford: 2016) 159.
134 EIA Directive, Art. 7.

assessment requirements laid out in Articles 5–10.[135] None of those projects seems to match sea-based measures, however.

2.5 Legal Categorization and Definition of Sea-Based Measures

2.5.1 General

There is a broad variety of techniques to reduce the leakage of phosphorus from the seabed, even among the purely 'technical' measures in focus in the present study.[136] Some of the techniques raise similar legal issues, while the legal implications of others need to be assessed on the basis of different legal instruments. In view of this, it is useful to establish certain main categories of measures depending on the type of measure as well as the type of legal challenges they raise. Three such categories have been identified here and will be further discussed, along with their main legal characteristics. The chosen categories are: dredging (subsection 2.5.2), chemical treatment (subsection 2.5.3), and oxygenation (subsection 2.5.4).

It should be kept in mind, though, that different measures may be regulated differently at different regulatory levels, and that some activities might be regulated at some levels but not at others. A general assumption for all categories is that, while the aim of taking sea-based measures is to combat eutrophication and improve the environmental status, these measures entail risks that trigger different environmental laws, principles, and protection obligations.

2.5.2 Dredging of Phosphorus-Rich Sediment

The first category of methods involves the dredging of phosphorus-rich sediment with the intention to eliminate phosphorus stored in the sediment. This method seeks to remove sediments from the seabed. Dredging is an activity that is generally unregulated by international legal instruments and regimes. UNCLOS is the only international instrument that has some express reference to dredging, requiring states to take necessary measures to ensure the protection of the marine environment in the international seabed area (the Area) from harmful effects of, *inter alia*, dredging.[137] This rule is not directly applicable in the Baltic Sea since it applies to the seabed beyond the limits of national jurisdiction, or the Area, and the Baltic Sea is covered by national continental shelves. A corresponding general obligation applies, however, through the more general environmental obligations of states in UNCLOS Part XII. Apart

---

135 EIA Directive, Art. 4(1).

136 This study does not cover natural measures such as fisheries, mussel farming, etc., but concentrates on the technical measures.

137 UNCLOS, Art. 145. See also Art. 17(2)(f) of Annex III.

COMBATTING EUTROPHICATION IN THE BALTIC SEA 37

from that, dredging clearly falls among the sovereign rights that states have over their continental shelves under Article 77(1).

The Helsinki Convention does not specifically mention dredging either. It regulates the exploration or exploitation of the seabed and other offshore activities with the aim to prevent pollution of the marine environment from such activities, but this primarily concerns the production or extraction of gas and oil.[138]

While dredging as such is not regulated internationally, the treatment of the dredged material is subject to a number of rules at regional (and national) level. The disposal of dredged materials is covered by the rules of the Helsinki Convention, which provides an exemption from the general dumping prohibition for dredged materials, but even in the case of dumping of such materials, strict requirements regarding permits and other precautions are set out in Annex V.[139]

However, as the purpose of dredging in the present context is to remove the sediment without returning the dredged materials to the sea, this regulation does not apply. It may be worth mentioning, however, that the effects of dredging and dumping of such materials in some aspects are comparable, e.g. as regards turbidity. On this basis, it has been suggested that if dumping of dredged materials is restricted, the dredging activity itself should also be undertaken with corresponding caution and restrictions.[140]

Beyond the direct risks that dredging might create for flora or fauna in the seabed, dredging may also entail adverse effects for the marine ecosystem because of the temporary increases in turbidity of sediment and the risk of the release of contaminants to the water column.[141] Because of this, dredging potentially invokes a number of more general environmental laws and principles and could very well fall within the definition of 'pollution of the marine environment' in UNCLOS and other instruments.[142]

---

138 Helsinki Convention, Art. 12.

139 Helsinki Convention, Art. 11. In 2015, HELCOM adopted revised Guidelines for Management of Dredged Material at Sea.

140 Swedish Environmental Protection Agency (Naturvårdsverket), Report, *Muddring och hantering av muddermassor: Vägledning om tillämpning av 11 och 15 kap Miljöbalken*, Miljörättsavdelningen 2010-02-18, 34ff. [in Swedish].

141 Swedish Environmental Protection Agency (Naturvårdsverket), Rapport 5999, *Miljöeffekter vid muddring och dumpning: En litteratursammanställning*, October 2009 [in Swedish].

142 See in particular, the significance attached to damage caused by dredging (admittedly at a different scale) by the arbitrational tribunal in the *South China Sea Arbitration*, https://pcacases.com/web/sendAttach/2086), paras. 978–983. In para. 983, the Tribunal concluded that "through its construction activities, China has breached its obligation under Article 192 to protect and preserve the marine environment, has conducted

EU law does not provide any specific regulation on dredging either, although it is indirectly within the scope of the water/marine framework directives which regulate the environmental quality status of waters, irrespective of the activity involved. In addition, if the dredged materials are considered to be waste – perhaps also including toxic substances or other forms of contaminants that are stored in the sediment – with the only purpose to be disposed of or stored, the regime for waste comes into play. This includes a variety of requirements relating to the disposal, permits, procedures, etc., which are mainly regulated by EU law and, through that, in national implementing legislation.[143]

If the activity is taken in coastal waters (within 1 nm from the baseline), the WFD applies. This means that the environmental objectives of the WFD have to be taken into account, and at a national level this could also include environmental quality standards (EQS).[144] Moreover, the WFD's principle of non-deterioration would then also be relevant.[145] As was noted above, the extension of the non-deterioration principle was the key question in the *Weser* case at the CJEU, which also significantly restricted the extent to which such activities can be pursued. The Court ruled that any activity – specifically dredging – leading to deterioration is prohibited, even if the deterioration only affects one of the environmental quality elements and even only on a temporary basis.[146]

A question that arises in the context of sea-based measures is whether and how the intentions behind the activity affect the application of this rule, and whether the environmental impact shall be considered in relation to the potential long-term environmental benefits of the activity or only through the short-term environmental impact. This issue is discussed further in Part 3 below.

2.5.3 Chemical Treatment

The use of chemicals to fixate the phosphorus in the sediment is the second category identified. The underlying idea here is to treat the seabed with certain

---

dredging in such a way as to pollute the marine environment with sediment in breach of Article 194(1), and has violated its duty under Article 194(5) to take measures necessary to protect and preserve rare or fragile ecosystems as well as the habitat of depleted, threatened or endangered species and other forms of marine life."

143 Regulated in Directive 2008/98/EC on waste (Waste Framework Directive).

144 See, e.g. section 4.2.3 below for the Swedish system and section 4.2.2 for the Finnish regulation on state of water and the classification of the water.

145 WFD, Art. 4.

146 Case C-461/13 Bund v Germany (the *Weser* Case). See also Common Implementation Strategy for the Water Framework Directive and the Floods Directive, Guidance Doc no 36, 21–22, where the time span is defined in different terms.

COMBATTING EUTROPHICATION IN THE BALTIC SEA

chemicals, such as aluminum, which bind the phosphorus to the sediment so that it cannot leak into the water, even in anoxic conditions. Other materials that could be used for the purpose include marl, mineral clay, or iron.[147] The environmental effects of these substances differ and different chemicals will entail different risks for the ecosystem. The legal assessment depends on the environmental effects and may hence be different depending on the substance used. However, the techniques for treatment and their legal attributes are similar, which means that they may be categorized together.

In this case, too, the starting point is an essentially permissive framework in which states have exclusive jurisdiction over the exploitation of their national waters and EEZ/continental shelf and to authorize and control marine scientific research in these areas. However, the general obligation to have due regard to the interest of other states apply along with the general obligations to protect the marine environment and prevent pollution.

As opposed to dredging, chemical treatment involves the introduction of substances into the sea, which not only potentially falls within the definition of marine pollution of UNCLOS, but also raises the question of whether it could be considered to represent dumping at sea.

In the London Convention, and in the London Protocol, dumping means, *inter alia*, "any deliberate disposal at sea of wastes or other matter from vessels, aircraft, platforms or other man-made structures at sea".[148] The same definition is found in UNCLOS and in the Helsinki Convention.[149] The term 'disposal' is not legally defined, but given that ocean fertilization has been considered to come under the scope of the London Convention and Protocol,[150] it is by no means excluded that chemical treatment of the seabed would be covered too. While chemicals deliberately used for the purpose of fixating phosphorus to the sediment would probably not represent 'waste' under this definition, they may still be considered dumping to the extent it falls under the notion of 'other matter'.

Another key question in this regard relates to the purpose of the placing of the matter in the sea. Both the London Convention and the Protocol provide that "placement of matter for a purpose other than the mere disposal thereof" is excluded from the scope of dumping, "provided that such placement is not contrary to the aims of [the] Convention [Protocol]."[151] A similar exception

---

147   For a summary of technologies and substances, see Vahanen Environment Oy and Centrum Balticum, 2018, chapter 3.3.1.
148   London Convention, Art. III(1)(a); London Protocol, Art. 1(4)(1)(1).
149   UNCLOS, Art. 1(5)(a)(i); Helsinki Convention, Art. 2(4)(a)(i).
150   Resolution LC-LP (2008), para. 1.
151   London Convention, Art. III (1)(b)(ii); London Protocol, Art. 1(4)2(2)).

is found also in the Helsinki Convention.[152] Since the purpose of chemical treatment is not "mere disposal" of the chemicals in question, this exemption may accordingly be used for excluding the activity from the dumping regime altogether, provided that it is not contrary to the aims of the conventions or protocol.

What, then, are the aims of the conventions? The general objective of the London Convention is for states to control pollution and thus, as part of this, to prevent dumping of wastes or other matter into the sea if it is "liable to create hazards to human health, to harm living resources and marine life, to damage amenities or to interfere with other legitimate uses of the sea."[153] The Helsinki Convention does not include a similar general article to declare its objective, but it follows from the text that the objectives of that convention is somewhat broader in that it also includes protection of intrinsic natural values including to "conserve natural habitats and biological diversity and to protect ecological processes".[154] The applicability of the dumping obligations to chemical treatment accordingly depends on the effects, including the environmental effects, of such measures. The greater risk for the marine environment they constitute, the more likely it is that they will be considered to be contrary to the aims of the conventions and hence included in the scope of dumping, independently of whether or not the purpose is to dispose of the chemicals. Depending on the substances used and the scientific basis for their use, it cannot be excluded that release of chemicals into the marine environment entails some level of risk and could thus be seen as both dumping and pollution of the marine environment (see section 3.2.2 below).

Even if an activity falls within the definition of dumping, it does not necessarily follow that it is ruled out. The London Convention only prohibits dumping of wastes or other matters that are listed in its Annex I. Wastes or other matters listed in Annex II requires a special permit, while wastes and other matters that are not included in the list only require a general permit. Depending on the substance chosen for chemical treatment, the Convention thus limits most dumping to become a question of a permit procedure. A special permit means permission granted specifically on application.[155] Both permit procedures require an advance application, but the permit procedure is

---

152 Helsinki Convention, Art. 2(4)b(ii).
153 London Convention, Art I.
154 Helsinki Convention, Art. 15. See also Art. 3(1): "The Contracting Parties shall individually or jointly take all appropriate legislative, administrative or other relevant measures to prevent and eliminate pollution in order to promote the ecological restoration of the Baltic Sea Area and the preservation of its ecological balance."
155 London Convention, Art. III(5).

COMBATTING EUTROPHICATION IN THE BALTIC SEA

more stringent for Annex II substances that require "special care". Neither aluminum nor clay, which for the time being represent the main sediment-treating substances of interest, are listed in any of the Annexes and thus treatment of the seabed with those chemicals would be subject to more permissive general permit according to the London Convention. However, Annex II does make a reference to "materials which, though of a non-toxic nature, may become harmful due to the quantities in which they are dumped, or which are liable to seriously reduce amenities."

However, under the London Protocol, which applies in five of the nine coastal states in the Baltic Sea, the regime is different. The London Protocol reverses the listing by establishing a general prohibition of dumping, with the exception of wastes and other matters listed in its Annex I. Neither aluminum nor iron is listed in the Annex, but it does provide for the issue of permits in respect of "inert, inorganic, geological material" and "organic material of natural origin", which again highlights the difference that applies depending on what material is used. Even the matters listed are only allowed if a permit is granted and they shall be subject to the permit procedures set out in Annex II. In addition, it is stated that any alternative to dumping that is more environmentally preferable shall be used as a first choice.[156] As a starting point, therefore, the Protocol rules out the introduction of aluminum or iron, to the extent the matter falls within the definition of dumping in the first place, which in turn depends on whether or not the activity is contrary to the aims of the Protocol.

The London Protocol also includes "any storage of wastes or other matter in the seabed and the subsoil thereof" within the definition of dumping.[157] This takes the concept of dumping further, but an amendment adopted in 2006 permits so-called permanent carbon sequestration under the seabed under certain prerequisites.[158] Carbon sequestration is included among the matters approved for dumping with a permit, found in Annex I. The aim of this is to reduce atmospheric CO_2 emissions from different industrial sources.[159] This represents a rare example of a case where one form of dumping has been approved for the purpose of protecting the environment in other ways.

However, other climate mitigation measures that classify as dumping have been rejected under the London Protocol. A particularly relevant example is

---

156 London Protocol, Art. 4(1).
157 London Protocol, Art. 1(4)(3).
158 Amendment to include CO_2 sequestration in sub-seabed geological formations in Annex 1 to the London Protocol Adopted on 2 November 2006, by Resolution LP.1(1), see circular LC-LP.1/Circ.5.
159 Birnie, Boyle and Redgwell, 2009, 468.

ocean fertilization for mitigation of climate change. Such measures have not been accepted within the frame of the Protocol, with reference to the precautionary approach laid down in the Protocol.[160] However, a framework for assessing ocean fertilization for research purposes has been developed and adopted, which allows such measures to be carried out under certain conditions. The measures suggested to reduce the amount of phosphorus in the Baltic Sea include certain important similarities to such geoengineering activities, which will be discussed in more detail in section 3.3.3.

In EU law, there are no rules specifically regulating dumping, though the EU is a party to UNCLOS, the London Convention, the London Protocol, and to the Helsinki Convention, all of which include prohibitions of dumping. Like with the case of dredging, the risks involved with the chemical treatment of the seabed raise matters linked to the WFD, and in particular the *Weser* case, evoking the non-deterioration principle. The prohibition that the *Weser* case establishes against activities causing any deterioration of the WFD classification indicators suggests that risks of chemical treatment of the seabed might very well be an obstacle to such measures too if performed in an area where the WFD is applicable.

2.5.4 Oxygenation

Oxygenation of the seabed by pumping more oxygenated water from the surface to further depths with the purpose of oxygenating the seabed is the third main category of sea-based measures that have been identified within the scope of the study. Oxygenation is a technique that does not immediately resemble any other activities at sea as regulated by international law. The underlying intention is that by adding oxygen or oxygen-rich water at a level close to the seabed, the chemical processes that bind phosphorus to the sediment can be restored while at the same time it helps to speed up the process of degrading of excess plants and algae.[161]

In practice, oxygenation differs from the other categories in that it is a long-term activity and requires a semi-permanent installation. While skimming and chemical treatment are one-off interventions, oxygenation is an on-going process which is likely to continue for months or years and will hence have long-term implications both for the environment and for other users of the sea.

---

160 London Protocol, Art. 3(1); Resolution LC-LP.1(2008) on the Regulation of Ocean Fertilization, adopted on the Thirtieth Meeting of the Contracting Parties to the London Convention and the Third Meeting of the Contracting Parties to the London Protocol; see also Sands and Peel, 2012, 396.

161 Vahanen Environment Oy and Centrum Balticum, 2018, 52 and 54–60.

Oxygenation also differs from the other methods in that it is not as easy to categorize in the existing legal framework. Pumping oxygen-rich water from one part of the sea to another does not fit within the definitions of dumping as discussed above. It does not involve any disposal of waste or other matter, and it is similarly doubtful that it involves "placement of matter for a purpose other than the mere disposal thereof", which could invoke the question of compatibility with the aims of the London Convention. It is accordingly difficult to apply the rules for dumping as such to oxygenation.

By contrast, oxygenation does represent "introduction by man, directly or indirectly, of substances or energy into the marine environment" and could hence represent 'pollution of the marine environment' under the definition in UNCLOS Article 1(4), to the extent that the activity "results or is likely to result in ... deleterious effects". This matter is reverted to in section 3.2.2 below.

Moreover, oxygenation clearly represents a "deliberate intervention in the marine environment to manipulate natural processes" and could hence fall within the definition of 'marine geoengineering' which was adopted under the London Protocol in 2013 but is not yet in force. Whether this means that the London Protocol framework for assessments would be applicable is not certain, as it is not clear whether geoengineering measures also need to qualify as "placement of matter" and considered to be against the purpose of the convention to fall within the scope of the regime. In the end, this issue will be decided by the contracting parties to the Protocol. The significance of the 'geoengineering' rules of the London Protocol for sea-based measures more generally is discussed below in section 3.3.3.

The absence of an international legal framework dealing with or covering oxygenation leaves the matter subject to the more general provisions of UNCLOS and other instruments on the protection and preservation of the marine environment, together with the environmental law principles which provide guidance on the balancing of interests involved.

Apart from those general environmental rules, which mainly address the environmental and other impacts of the circulation of water that the technology entails, the legal framework also includes rules on the installation as such. Oxygenation requires technical equipment that is placed in the ocean, presumably tied to the seabed in some way, and that needs to be supplied with energy. The construction and maintenance of such installations are regulated in UNCLOS.

The technical construction necessary for the operation of oxygenation measures appears to fall squarely within the scope of the term "installation or structure" as regulated by, but not defined in, UNCLOS. In the absence of a definition, the boundaries of the concept can be sought in relation to other activities and constructions that are specifically regulated, such as artificial islands, submarine cables, and pipelines. Jurisdiction-wise, UNCLOS provides that in the EEZ and on the continental shelf, the coastal states have the exclusive right to authorize and regulate the construction, operation and use of, *inter alia*, installations and structures.[162] The only limitations or restrictions to the construction or operation of an installation are the general environmental principles, the requirements found in Part XII of UNCLOS, and that such installation cannot interfere with the recognized sea lanes essential to international navigation. A safety zone of maximum 500 meters may, where necessary, be established around such installations to ensure the safety of navigation and of the installation itself. There is also an established duty to notify where such an installation is and to remove it after its use.[163] In brief, this regime places certain obligations on the setting up and operation of such installations, but does not question the exclusive authority of the coastal state to establish and operate them in their EEZ and, *a fortiori*, their territorial sea.

The EU law that is applicable to oxygenation is again, at least to some extent, the general requirements on good environmental/ecological status found in the WFD and – for large-scale trials in the deep basins – the MSFD. Moreover, the Birds and the Habitats Directive may restrict the geographical areas where such installations could be allowed without a special permit.[164]

In this case, too, the conclusions of the *Weser* judgment regarding the non-deterioration principle would draw a rather strict line for what is permissible, if the WFD is applicable. The pumping process connected to the oxygenation seems, for example, to entail a risk of stirring effects. However, the WFD applies a range of quality indicators and it is possible that an oxygenation installation could have adverse effects on the environmental status also in other ways.

The MSFD, as was already noted, applies in all sea areas beyond the baseline, only overlapping the geographical scope of the WFD by 1 nm. The MSFD is not directly applicable to a specific activity or project. Instead, the MSFD functions as a steering mechanism for the overall approach taken by the member states in their planning and managing of land-use and water areas at a general level. The indicators and status classifications made in relation to the MSFD are also at a larger scale and are not specific to single effects on a limited area. It is not clear, therefore, that the logic of the *Weser* case could be transposed

---

162 UNCLOS, Art. 60; and regarding jurisdiction for installations on the continental shelf, see Art. 80.
163 UNCLOS, Art. 60.
164 Habitats Directive, Art. 6.

COMBATTING EUTROPHICATION IN THE BALTIC SEA 45

to this setting.[165] Rather, the wider question is whether the potential positive effects of sea-based measures could also have effects for the purpose and goal of good environmental status according to the MSFD.

2.6 *Summary*

The above review of the applicable international legal framework indicates that different types of sea-based measures may give rise to somewhat different legal questions. First, the technology used to prevent the phosphorus from leaking from the bottom sediments affects the legal framework. Different laws and legal assessments apply (at least to some extent) to the different types of measures, highlighting the relationship between different types of measures and the rules for dumping, installations, etc.

In addition, it follows that the rights and obligations related to undertaking such measures, at least to some extent, depend on the geographical location of the measures. Different laws apply in the different jurisdictional zones, which affects the applicability of international law as well as national legislation. Perhaps surprisingly, the spatial categorization indicates that EU law currently appears to have a stronger impact on the applicable rights and obligations than the law of the sea and that the critical limit in this respect is 1 nautical mile from the baseline as introduced by the WFD, as implemented by subsequent case law, notably the *Weser* judgment by the CJEU. Within the 1 nm limit, the WFD applies, with some complementary requirements of the MSFD, while outside the limit, the rules of the MSFD apply.

In an effort to summarize the legal review in a single picture, Table 1 below indicates the most relevant international and EU laws that apply for different measures in different areas.

Table 1 illustrates that some differences exist with respect to the laws that apply to the different measures, e.g. that the EU waste legislation and international dumping regime apply to chemical treatment, but not to dredging and oxygenation measures. It also illustrates that the relevant spatial limits for determining the relevant laws differ between EU law and international law. While international law, in this case, provides for unusually extensive regulation for states to apply within their internal waters, mainly through the provisions of the Helsinki Convention, the baseline forming the border between internal waters and the territorial sea still represents a key borderline for the applicability of international vis-à-vis national rules. In EU law, by contrast, the relevant dividing line is the 1 nm zone from the baseline that

---

165   See section 2.3.4.3 above.

TABLE 1 Applicable rules of EU and international law in different sea areas for different categories of sea-based measures

		Chemical treatment	Oxygenation	Dredging
Internal waters	EU	WFD, Waste Proced.: EIA, Habitats/Birds	WFD Proced.: EIA, Habitats/Birds	WFD Proced.: EIA, Habitats/Birds
	International	LC/LP, HELCOM Espoo Conv.	HELCOM Espoo Conv.	HELCOM Espoo Conv.
Territorial sea	EU	(WFD 1 or 12 nm), MSFD, MSP, Waste Proced.: EIA, Habitats/Birds	(WFD 1 nm), MSFD, MSP Proced.: EIA, Habitats/Birds	(WFD 1 nm), MSFD, MSP Proced.: EIA, Habitats/Birds
	International	UNCLOS (principles, etc.) HELCOM, LC/LP, CBD Espoo Conv	UNCLOS (principles, innocent passage, etc.), HELCOM, CBD Espoo Conv	UNCLOS (principles, CS) HELCOM, CBD Espoo Conv
EEZ/CS	EU	MSFD, MSP Proced.: EIA, Habitats/Birds	MSFD, MSP Proced.: EIA, Habitats/Birds	MSFD, MSP, Waste Proced.: EIA, Habitats/Birds
	International	UNCLOS (CS, EEZ), HELCOM, LC, LP, CBD Espoo Conv.	UNCLOS (principles, due regard, installations), HELCOM, CBD Espoo Conv.	UNCLOS (principles, CS), HELCOM, CBD Espoo Conv.

determines the applicability between the two marine directives and has no basis in the law of the sea.

Yet, in the end, neither the substantive nor the geographical categorization appears decisive for defining the legal rights and obligations linked to sea-based measures. The rules referred to in the table only provide for certain general obligations and principles to be applied when their legality is assessed at a national level. None of the categories of measures can be ruled out or accepted without an assessment of the competing interests at stake, including the environmental impact of the measure.

The geographical categorization under the law of the sea (as reflected in UNCLOS) is not of crucial relevance either. This follows, on the one hand, from the complete coverage of the Baltic Sea by coastal zones of the littoral states and the availability of a fairly broad environmental jurisdiction for coastal states in any maritime zone, including the EEZ. On the other hand, it follows from the fact that the Helsinki Convention applies to all maritime zones, including the EEZ and internal waters of the states parties, which results in a rather similar regulatory situation independently of the coastal zone involved.

In order to proceed with the analysis of the legality of sea-based measures, it is thus relevant to study the extent to which international and EU law provide guidance on how the various interests at stake in sea-based measures should be balanced.

3 Key Issues Raised by Sea-Based Measures

3.1 *General*

A particular feature of sea-based measures is that the risks that they involve and their purpose relate to the same concern, i.e. the state of the marine environment. This convergence of concerns raises some additional questions relating to the applicability and role of certain key legal concepts and the balancing of the interests involved. Section 3.2 illustrates three cases where this convergence of concerns becomes legally relevant and where the risks of measures need to be balanced against their potential benefits. Firstly, it is assessed how sea-based measures might fit into the general duty of states to protect the marine environment (section 3.2.1); and, secondly, whether they qualify as 'pollution of the marine environment' which, in that case, brings along a number of consequential international obligations (section 3.2.2). Thirdly, the balancing of the environmental consequences of the measures is considered, notably on how the balance between the short-term risks and longer-term effects should be approached (section 3.2.3).

The examples illustrate that existing environmental legal rules and principles are largely based upon the assumption that information is available about technologies, alternatives, risks, and consequences. The environmental risks of an activity will, for example, be decisive for determining whether the activity is to be considered 'pollution of the marine environment', 'dumping', or 'marine geoengineering', all of which are key concepts for determining the rights and obligations involved. If the measures succeed in improving the environment without posing major short-term risks, the law presents few obstacles for their introduction. Conversely, if the benefits are limited and the environmental risks are important, a whole range of legal obstacles present themselves across all legal levels. Bluntly put, the legality of sea-based measures ultimately depends on whether or not they are effective in meeting their environmental objectives.

Another peculiarity with sea-based measures is the scientific uncertainty that surrounds them. The knowledge required for determining their risks and benefits – and hence the applicable legal constraints – is simply not available. While certain tests have been made with respect to some of the technologies, they have been small-scale operations and usually undertaken in very sheltered waters. For the rest, any calculation on their risks and benefits is based on laboratory and desktop estimations. In addition, as was noted in section 1.1, the outcome of such estimates, and even the results of the real-life experiments are disputed within the scientific community, notably by leading marine biologists.[166]

This state of affairs, in turn, prompts the question as to how environmental law deals with scientific uncertainty. The matter is addressed through general principles of environmental law, the most relevant of which are addressed in section 3.3.1. Particular attention is given to the precautionary principle (section 3.3.2), which is the only principle specifically developed for addressing scientific uncertainty. It is concluded that the ambiguities surrounding the meaning and impact of these principles limit them as a tool for providing general guidance and that the main obstacle inhibiting their implementation in the present case is the absence of knowledge about the effects of various kinds of sea-based measures. Further harmonization of their use seems desirable. That said, the principles may nevertheless be useful as they crystallize and clarify the values at stake, e.g. relating to the more specific regional or national approach to precaution and preventive action, or with respect to the level of scientific certainty or technology required.

A relatively recent example of how a corresponding situation of significant scientific uncertainty has been addressed in the framework of the London Dumping regime is discussed in section 3.3.3. The regulatory response to marine geoengineering measures, notably in the form of ocean fertilization, could provide an interesting blueprint for the tools available for regulators in the Baltic Sea.

3.2 Convergence of Concerns: Regulatory Relevance

3.2.1 The Duty to Protect the Marine Environment

While states have extensive rights to use their waters and resources, those rights need to be exercised in light of, and with due regard to, the rights of

---

166   See note 5 above.

other states. The principle that states shall not permit their territory or operations under their jurisdiction to harm the interests of other states or to territories beyond their jurisdiction (the 'no harm' principle) is the most basic and long-standing principle of international environmental law. It has since been supplemented by the principle of prevention which is not limited to transboundary harm. However, the principles do not imply a duty to prevent *any* environmental harm but only an obligation to exercise due diligence to that end. It is a duty to take the preventive steps, not an obligation of result. Potential harm must be taken into account if it is significant, but need not be serious or irreversible.[167] The duty of diligence varies but is commonly considered to be more severe for riskier activities.[168] More elaborate duties to protect and prevent harm to the marine environment follow from the obligations in UNCLOS and the Helsinki Convention.

The obligation in UNCLOS to protect the marine environment extends to all sea areas, including the states' own waters, and hence represents a limitation of the general right of states to exercise full sovereignty over their waters. The obligation moreover applies independently of any harm to other states. It is a duty to protect the environment for its own sake, its own intrinsic value. Here, too, it is an obligation of conduct, i.e. to take preventive measures.

The Helsinki Convention, on its part, requires that states "... individually or jointly take all appropriate legislative, administrative or other relevant measures to prevent and eliminate pollution in order to promote the ecological restoration of the Baltic Sea Area and the preservation of its ecological balance."[169] This clarifies some aspects of the due diligence obligation of states and places specific emphasis on the ecological effects of their action or inaction. The measures referred to are further clarified in other articles of the convention and in its annexes.

In assessing the more precise meaning of the obligation to protect or the appropriateness and relevance of sea-based measures, a specific challenge is that the obligations may work both ways in their guidance on whether such measures should be permitted. On the one hand, the duty could entail restrictions on the operation of such measures, in any sea area, due to concerns related to the environmental effects of the measure. On the other hand, it could also be understood as an obligation to actively take such measures in order to protect the marine environment from the threats of eutrophication. Either way, it seems clear that applying the environmental protection duty to sea-based

---

167   *Pulp Mills on the River Uruguay* (Argentina v. Uruguay), para. 101.
168   SDC ITLOS Case No. 17, para. 117.
169   Helsinki Convention, Art. 3(1).

measures necessarily involves a balancing between the environmental risks and benefits, both short-term and long-term, of the measure in question.

The outcome of such an assessment depends on a variety of factors, such as the benefits of the activity, the availability of other mechanisms to achieve the same results and how they compare in terms of effectiveness, cost and environmental risk. If equally effective measures exist, but at lower environmental risk or cost, it will be more difficult to argue for the appropriateness of sea-based measures.

In sum, it is difficult to conclude on the relevance of even the most basic environmental obligations for sea-based measures, as any assessment presupposes the availability of comprehensive information about the measure, its risks, and available alternatives. This, in turn, suggests that the matter has to be approached on a case-by-case basis and that the duty to protect the marine environment may come to play a different role depending on the measure in question and on the sea area and circumstances involved. Since, as is explained in Part 4 below, the balancing of interests will normally be undertaken at national or even sub-national level, the current legal framework entails obvious risks of fragmentation in the form of different opinions and interpretations in different Baltic Sea countries.

3.2.2 Could Sea-Based Measures be Characterized as Pollution?

Another crucial question for assessing the legality of sea-based measures is whether the activity in question is to be regarded as 'pollution of the marine environment' or 'dumping', both of which in that case would trigger a series of consequential obligations.[170] Here, too, the assessment essentially depends on the level of environmental risk stemming from the activity.

All sea-based measures discussed here include certain environmental risks, albeit the magnitude of the risk varies from one technique to another. Treating the seabed with chemicals entails risks of pollution and deterioration in the chemical status, the significance of which depends on the substance used. Research indicates, for example, that the level of free aluminum in the ecosystem and in the fish stock rises after conducting such treatment, even if the levels also tend to normalize rather fast.[171] Other substances, like clay,

---

170 It should be noted, though, that states are bound by a number of environmental obligations, including the no-harm principle and the general obligation to protect the marine environment and fragile ecosystems, even if the activity in question is not classified as pollution.

171 E. Rydin et al., 'Remediation of a Eutrophic Bay in the Baltic Sea', in *Environmental Science and Technology* (vol. 51, no. 8: 2017); E. Rydin and L. Kumblad, *Ecologically relevant phosphorus in coastal sediments*, HELCOM-EUSBSR Workhop in Göteborg 28.–29.11.2017.

COMBATTING EUTROPHICATION IN THE BALTIC SEA

may involve considerably smaller risks. For dredging, or skimming the seabed, it has similarly been observed that the activity may cause e.g. turbidity of the sediment, but the longer-term effects are not well understood.[172] Turbidity may affect the life in the sea primarily through reduced visibility and light and due to the release of toxic substances from historic pollution tied to the sediment. The environmental risks involved with oxygenation have also been highlighted,[173] and in this case, the risks are clearly long-term in view of the continuous nature of the operation. However, for all three techniques, it remains true that the long-term risks and potential effects on the marine ecosystem in a wider perspective are significantly under-studied, in particular as regards larger scale operations. The establishment of the polluting characteristics of various sea-based measures is therefore coupled with serious challenges from a purely scientific perspective. This also affects the determination of whether the measures represent pollution in a legal sense.

The legal assessment of whether or not the different sea-based measures should be characterized as pollution is complicated by the absence of any guidance on the severity of the environmental harm that constitutes pollution in the relevant instruments. Nevertheless, some guidance on how the matter should be approached follows directly from the definitions. First, neither the definition of 'pollution of the marine environment' nor of 'dumping' include any transboundary element, which means that harm to the marine environment in any sea area will suffice for falling within the scope of the

---

172   A. Sarvilinna and I. Sammalkorpi, *Rehevöityneen järven kunnostus ja hoito* (*Restoration and management of eutrophic lakes*) (Environment Guide, Finnish Environment Institute: 2010) [in Finnish]; G. Newcombe et al., *Management Strategies for Cyanobacteria (Blue-Green Algae): A Guide for Water Utilities* (Research Report No 74, CRF for Water Quality and Treatment: 2010).

173   The most long-term research projects of this kind in the Baltic Sea are the PROPPEN project in Sandöfjärden, Sweden and Lännerstasundet, Finland (see E. Rantajärvi (ed.) et.al., *Controlling benthic release of phosphorus in different Baltic Sea scales. Final Report on the result of the PROPPEN Project (802-0301-08) to the Swedish Environmental Protection Agency, Formas and VINNOVA* (Finnish Environmental Institute: 2012)) and the BOX project in Byfjord, Sweden (A. Stigebrandt et al., 'Consequences of artificial deepwater ventilation in the Bornholm Basin for oxygen conditions, cod reproduction and benthic biomass – A model study', in *Ocean Science* (vol. 11: 2015a) 93–110). Results also published in e.g. A. Stigebrandt and O. Kalén, 'Improving oxygen conditions in the deeper parts of the Bornholm Sea by pumped injection of winter water', in *Ambio* (vol. 42, no. 5: 2013) 587–595; A. Stigebrandt et al., 'A new phosphorus paradigm for the Baltic Proper', in *Ambio* (vol. 43: 2014) 634–643; A. Stigebrandt et al., 'An experiment with forced oxygenation of the deep-water of the anoxic By Fjord, western Sweden', in *Ambio* (vol. 44: 2015b) 42–54; and A. Stigebrandt, 'On the response of the Baltic Proper to changes of the total phosphorus supply', in *Ambio* (vol. 47: 2018) 31–44.

definition. In relation to dumping, the critical criteria for any "placement of a matter other than the mere disposal thereof" is whether or not it is "contrary to the aims of the Convention (or Protocol)".[174] The main aim of the Dumping Convention/Protocol that this criteria refers to is to "prevent the pollution of the sea by ... matter that is liable to create hazards to human health, to harm living resources and marine life ...".[175] Second, the definitions do not qualify the level of harm by additional requirements, such as 'significant' damage or threat of 'irreversible' damage, etc. Merely harming the environment suffices and this harm may, under Article 1(4), take different shapes, including "harm to living resources and marine life, ... hindrance to marine activities ... and other legitimate uses of the sea ... and reduction of amenities". Moreover, under both definitions, potential harm to the environment suffices, as it is enough that the activities concerned are "liable" or "likely" to bring about harmful effects. Similar wording is used in the definition of geoengineering in the amendment of the London Protocol. In other words, a mere risk of harmful effects triggers the definitions and it is enough that the harm is likely to occur. Conversely, to remain outside the scope of these definitions, environmental harm should be considered to be unlikely, which appears to be challenging in light of existing knowledge.

The extent to which the purpose behind the measure affects their legal characterization differs between the wordings of the different international instruments. While the definition of dumping appears to give a certain significance to the aim of the activity, the definition of pollution of the marine environment in UNCLOS and other instruments is neutral with respect to the intention behind the actions. If the definition is neutral, the placing of the substance in the sea for the purpose of long-term environmental benefits would not affect its status as pollution.

On this basis, it seems prudent to assume that the sea-based measures discussed here fall under the definition of pollution to the marine environment. This does not in itself rule out that such activities are permitted, but brings along a range of obligations in UNCLOS and other instruments that specifically relate to pollution.[176]

3.2.3 Long-Term vs Short-Term Environmental Effects

Sea-based measures play a potentially significant role in reducing eutrophication in the Baltic Sea, but as was noted above, none of the measures are entirely

---

174 London Convention, Art. III(1)(b).
175 London Convention, Art. I.
176 E.g. UNCLOS, Arts. 194(2) and (4), 195, 199, 204, and 205.

without environmental risk and the nature of the risks are often uncertain. Yet, in contrast to many other polluting activities which are typically advanced by economic interests, sea-based measures are introduced for the benefit of the marine environment. Since the very purpose of sea-based measures is to improve the state of the marine environment, environmental rules, principles, and procedures cannot only be used for placing conditions and restrictions on such measures. The same rules and principles may very well work in the opposite direction as well, by constituting an argument and legal justification for undertaking such measures. Which of the arguments eventually prevails depends, once again, on the capacity of the measure in reality to meet its environmental objectives.

Even if, as was noted above, the definition of pollution does not take into account the intentions behind the measure, it thus seems obvious that the risks linked to the measures must be balanced against their intended environmental benefits. The question of how the risks are to be evaluated against benefits is particularly pertinent with respect to the measures that only require a very brief period of interference to be put in effect, i.e. dredging and chemical treatment of the seabed.

At an international law level, there is no known case law where the short-term and long-term effects of pollution have been balanced against each other, nor was this a relevant aspect in the *Weser* ruling by the CJEU.[177] The latter case, however, suggests that the deterioration of the environment is to be assessed independently, without regard to the purpose or even duration of the activity, as long as the activity is not specifically part of a long-term plan and subject to a derogation.

In the field of international prescription, relevant guidance could be sought through two ocean-related measures aimed at mitigating climate change that have been addressed within the framework of the London Dumping regime in the past decades.[178] The first example relates to the storage of carbon dioxide in the seabed while the other one concerns marine geoengineering measures. The outcome of the deliberations was different in the two cases. While carbon capture and storage was accepted, subject to certain rigorous procedures, marine geoengineering measures such as ocean fertilization were considered to be contrary to the aims of the convention, unless carried out for research purposes. In neither case did the environmental purpose of the measure (mitigating climate change) prove decisive in the discussions. While the uncertainty of the environmental effectiveness was noted in both cases,

---

177   See section 2.3.4.2 above.
178   See section 2.2.2 above.

not least in relation to the available means of measuring those effects, it was the effect and risk of the measure itself that guided the decision-makers to different solutions.[179]

The above suggests that there are no general principles in place to govern the balancing between the short-term and long-term impact of the measures. This needs to be reviewed individually in view of the available knowledge of the (short-term and long-term) risks and benefits involved. On the assumption that the long-term benefits are the same, it will obviously be easier to justify a measure with very limited proven risks over a very limited period of time, than a more uncertain technology that impacts the ecosystem for a long period.

A particular feature of sea-based measures in this respect, which differs from the traditional balancing between environmental and other interests, is that the benefits and risks involved essentially relate to the same concern, i.e. the ecological state of the marine environment. This commonality of concerns emphasizes the role of science in the overall assessment.

The main problem for anyone seeking to strike a balance between the interests involved is that there is little scientific knowledge available on both the risks and benefits of any of the sea-based measures discussed here. Since both the risks and benefits are uncertain, the legal framework will also be uncertain. An important issue is, therefore, to analyze how the law deals with such scientific uncertainty.

3.3 *Dealing with Uncertainties: the Role of Environmental Principles*

3.3.1 Relevant Environmental Law Principles

Environmental law is primarily focused on providing rules on prevention and protection against environmental harm. These types of rules presuppose some knowledge on the risks and/or dangers linked to a certain activity or measure. Since risks and dangers are not always easy to foresee and may change over time, international environmental law provides a number of general principles with a more flexible role to ensure regulatory proactivity and precaution in relation to the changing environment.[180]

---

179 See K. N. Scott, 'Geoengineering and the Marine Environment', in R. Rayfuse (ed.), *Research Handbook on International Marine Environmental Law* (Edward Elgar Publishing, Cheltenham: 2015) 458–461; and P. Williamson et al., 'Ocean fertilization for geoengineering: A review of effectiveness, environmental impacts and emerging governance', in *Process Safety and Environmental Protection* (vol. 90, no. 6: 2012) 475–488.

180 Sands and Peel, 2012, 187ff. Many of the principles are also listed in the Treaty on the Functioning of the European Union, Art. 191, as guiding principles for the EU's environmental policy.

The most well-known environmental principles are the 'No-harm Principle', the 'Precautionary Principle', the principle of 'Preventive Action', 'Polluter Pays Principle', 'Best Available Technique', 'Best Environmental Practice', and the 'Ecosystem Approach' to governance. These principles are commonly used for establishing a balance between the risks and benefits of certain activities, by means of general guidance rather than precise operational rules. Their application will always be related to the individual situation. Different principles target different levels of risk and environmental uncertainty.

If an activity is potentially causing environmental harm outside the national territory and the risk of that is relatively well understood, the no-harm principle applies. The principle of preventive action, on its part, requires the prevention of damage to the environment, including within national borders, or, otherwise, to reduce, limit, or control harmful activities. In addition, there is also an obligation for states to adopt appropriate measures for the prevention of harm. The precautionary principle is not limited to transboundary damage either but applies at an earlier stage of risk. It applies when the risk is only likely, even if it is not an established fact. The purpose of the precautionary principle is that the lack of scientific certainty in relation to the risks involved shall not be used as a reason to postpone cost-effective measures that may prevent environmental degradation, or even stop the planned activity altogether.[181] Hence, this principle is the most immediate limitation to any potentially harmful actions and activities.[182]

The purpose of the polluter pays principle is different. The aim is such that the costs associated with the pollution should be paid by those responsible for it, thereby also generating a preventive effect. These costs could be both those connected to preventive measures as well as the costs of remedying the environment if it has been harmed by the pollution.

The other environmental law principles mentioned, primarily the principles of best available technique and best environmental practice, but to some extent also the ecosystem approach, apply where the assumption is that the activities do not pose an imminent threat to the environment. Hence, the activities should generally be allowed but should be performed with the greatest care, taking into account any potential environmental degradation that may entail. The environmental risk or scientific uncertainty targeted by these principles relate to governance and management measures or technical developments. Based on the current level of knowledge, they assume an adaptive approach, continuously integrating new knowledge into the activities. In this

---

181   See further in, e.g., Sands and Peel, 2012, 217ff.

182   *Ibid.*, 200–203.

way, monitoring of the activities is sufficient as a safeguard against risks and the principles ensure that changes of the status quo or in the scientific knowledge will always be taken into account and enhance the level of prevention in the measures taken.

The ecosystem approach is more of a concept or legal approach for implementing adaptive management and regulation, rather than a principle in the above sense. Yet, it may also provide guidance on where to focus when balancing the risks. It can also serve as a tool for applying the precautionary principle in a new setting, as part of a management approach of ecosystems, in the absence of complete knowledge. One main purpose of the ecosystem approach, as it has been developed in the legal context, is that it is necessary to create sustainable structures for management despite a lack of full knowledge and that the design of these structures shall be founded on ecosystem dynamics and thus need to be adaptive.[183]

All these principles are of relevance for sea-based measures and will serve to guide decision-makers in the process of whether or not to authorize a given sea-based measure. The environmental law principles have differing legal status; while some are well established as part of the corpus of international law, some are strongly implemented through EU law and others have a generally more debated legal status. It is significant that all of them, at least in some measure, are found in the Helsinki Convention or its annexes, which means that they apply as binding law throughout the Baltic Sea.[184] However, also in the case where the environmental law principles cannot be identified as directly applicable through international conventions or EU laws, they may still be applicable at a national level. The key environmental law principles are often implemented at a national level and hence guide the national procedures for permits and other national restrictions that the activities discussed here are subject to.[185]

In view of the scientific uncertainties linked to sea-based measures, the application of the precautionary principle is particularly relevant and will be discussed separately in the next section. Apart from that, sea-based measures seem to fall somewhat in-between the scope and coverage of these principles. They are not posing obvious threats to the environment – within or beyond national borders – to the extent that they should be prohibited on the basis

---

183 See, e.g. A. K. Nilsson and B. Bohman, 'Legal prerequisites for ecosystem-based management in the Baltic Sea area: The example of eutrophication', in *Ambio* (vol. 44, sup. 3: 2015) 371.

184 Helsinki Convention, Art. 3(2).

185 See section 4.2 below.

COMBATTING EUTROPHICATION IN THE BALTIC SEA

of the no-harm principle or the principle of preventive action. Moreover, the potential consequences of different types of sea-based measures are not sufficiently clarified for applying preventive measures. How to assess the best available technique or best environmental practice in this context is also up for debate – should they be assessed in light of the current research on sea-based measures or should the matter also be reviewed in relation to land-based measures to curb eutrophication? Is the best available technique sufficiently safe at this stage of development? The polluter pays principle would mostly be relevant in relation to placing potential responsibility for pollution or other damage on the operators of sea-based measures. On the other hand, the purpose of sea-based measures is to reduce the internal load of phosphorus that comes from past polluting activities, which opens up for an application of the same principles in their favour. Whether sea-based measures could be regarded as the necessary preventive measure to mitigate damage caused by past polluters depends, *inter alia*, on their consequences which, again, leads to the question of their factual effect.

Ultimately the assessment of how the environmental law principles operate in the context of sea-based measures will be left to the national authorities in their permit procedures, and possibly under more specific guidance from HELCOM in the future. It may be noted, though, that the growing significance attached to the ecosystem approach could be considered as a call for more dynamic perspectives on sea-based measures and their potential risks. In making the assessment, account should, in other words, be taken of the broader effects of the measures for the ecosystem as a whole rather than just focusing on the direct reduction of phosphorus and eutrophication.

3.3.2 The Precautionary Principle

The precautionary principle is designed precisely to deal with scientific uncertainties in relation to activities that may be harmful to the environment. The precise content of the principle is not settled, however, ranging from a 'weak' version, which triggers the principle only in cases of serious or irreversible damage and even then does not oblige the state to do anything,[186] to a 'strong' version that heavily leans towards preserving the status quo and places the burden of proving that there will be no environmental harm on the operator alone.[187] In view of this uncertainty, international courts, including the

---

186   United Nations Declaration on Environment and Development (adopted 16 June 1992) 31 ILM 1992 (the Rio Declaration) Principle 15.
187   World Charter for Nature, 1982, UN General Assembly, UNGA Res. 37/7, 22 ILM 455 (1983), Art. 11(b).

International Court of Justice (ICJ), have been reluctant to acknowledge the principle as forming part of customary law.[188]

For present purposes, it suffices to note that the principle is laid down in relatively similar terms in both the Helsinki Convention and the London Protocol.[189] The former definition reads:

> The Contracting Parties shall apply the precautionary principle, i.e., to take preventive measures when there is reason to assume that substances or energy introduced, directly or indirectly, into the marine environment may create hazards to human health, harm living resources and marine ecosystems, damage amenities or interfere with other legitimate uses of the sea even when there is no conclusive evidence of a causal relationship between inputs and their alleged effects.

The definition makes it clear that application of the principle is not facultative but that states shall apply preventive measures when a certain activity may harm the marine environment. The reference to the absence of conclusive evidence presupposes that some evidence exists to suggest that the activity is harmful, however, there is no certainty about the matter. The latter is regarded as the very core of the precautionary principle.

The definition, which applies to all sea areas, thus appears to cover the potential harm and scientific uncertainty that surrounds all sea-based measures discussed here. It suggests that states in these circumstances shall "take preventive measures", which in itself is unclear, but presumably involves significant restraints in authorizing the activity.

On the other hand, the environmental objectives of the measures need to be acknowledged here, too. It may be argued that the state of the eutrophication in the Baltic Sea, furthered by the ecosystem approach, requires further mitigation measures to be put in place and that all options to ameliorate the ecological state of the sea have to be examined. The precautionary approach should not, accordingly, be used as an excuse for not further exploring new options of interest. At the very least, the fact that there is a significant

---

188 E.g. ICJ Judgment in the Case Concerning *Pulp Mills on the River Uruguay* (Argentina v. Uruguay) of 20 April, 2010 ICJ Rep 14. However, a Special Chamber of the International Tribunal for the Law of the Sea in 2011 declared that the inclusion of Rio Principle 15 into several international conventions "has initiated a trend towards making this approach part of customary international law." SDC Adv Opinion, Case 17, para. 135.

189 Helsinki Convention, Art. 3(2), London Protocol, Art. 3(1). The precautionary principle is also mentioned in The Treaty on the Functioning of the European Union OJ C 326/47 (TFEU), Art. 191(2).

COMBATTING EUTROPHICATION IN THE BALTIC SEA 59

knowledge gap – which triggers the precautionary principle – should not be used as an excuse for not undertaking the kind of research that is necessary to gain that missing knowledge.[190]

The precautionary principle is operationalized by procedural tools, notably the obligations related to EIAs, which include an assessment of the overall risks and benefits prior to pursuing any activity that may cause significant damage. A number of related obligations seek to ensure that the state is well informed at the time of decision-making and that the uncertainty of the impact is reduced to a minimum.[191] In addition, various instruments call for a duty of states to monitor the environmental impact of activities under their jurisdiction.[192] Those obligations highlight the continuous nature of the state's obligations and, in particular, that the state's obligations do not end with the termination of the permit process.

Upon evaluation, it seems clear that international law in general, and the Helsinki Convention in particular, call for caution in approving activities wherein the full environmental effects are not yet known. The types of sea-based measures discussed here belong to this category, at least as far as larger scale or off-shore measures are concerned. This calls for a cautious approach in the national permit approval process across the whole range of measures. On the other hand, more knowledge about risks and benefits, including risks of non-action, cannot be obtained without the experience of the implementation of sea-based measures in practice. It seems clear, therefore, that while the precautionary approach may require the imposition of strict conditions on the operation of sea-based measures, it does not rule out the approval of projects aimed at learning more about their effects.

3.3.3 Addressing Geoengineering Measures at the London Dumping Regime – a Relevant Example?

The precautionary principle has not been applied to concrete questions under the Helsinki Convention, however, the London dumping regime has

---

190 V. Galaz, 'Geo-engineering, governance, and social-ecological systems: critical issues and joint research needs', in *Ecology and Society* (vol. 17, no. 1: 2012) 24, http://dx.doi.org/10.5751/ES-04677-170124; K. Güssow et al., 'Ocean iron fertilization: Why further research is needed', in *Marine Policy* (vol. 34, no. 5: 2010) 911–918.

191 See Parts 2.2.2 and 2.3.1 above.

192 UNCLOS, Art. 204(2) provides that "States shall keep under surveillance the effects of any activities which they permit or in which they engage in order to determine whether these activities are likely to pollute the marine environment" while Art. 6(3) of the Helsinki Convention provides that "Contracting Parties shall ensure that authorized emissions to water and air are monitored and controlled."

recently addressed a case concerning ocean geoengineering measures used to mitigate climate change. Even if the amendment to the London Protocol is not yet in force, it deserves to be assessed in more detail, as it represents an example of a way to balance the different risks and interests involved in novel measures to address environmental concerns and, hence, draws many parallels to sea-based measures.

The framework for dealing with geoengineering measures under the London Protocol has been developed to deal specifically with ocean fertilization to abate climate change, but may be extended to other geoengineering activities.[193] Even though sea-based measures, in many respects, have the opposite aim to that of ocean fertilization, as they seek to reduce – rather than increase – nutrients in the sea, the principal issues bear many similarities.

In this case, the parties to the London Convention first confirmed the applicability of the dumping regime to ocean fertilization. In a joint resolution in 2008, the governing bodies of the Convention and the Protocol established that "the scope of the London Convention and Protocol includes ocean fertilization activities".[194] Ocean fertilization was defined as "any activity undertaken by humans with the principal intention of stimulating primary productivity in the oceans."[195]

The resolution provided for a precautionary approach by stating that "given the present state of knowledge, ocean fertilization activities other than legitimate scientific research should not be allowed".[196] The parties further agreed that in order to provide for legitimate scientific research, and hence

---

193   The London Protocol defines marine geoengineering as the "deliberate intervention in the marine environment to manipulate natural processes, including to counteract anthropogenic climate change and/or its impacts, and that has the potential to result in deleterious effects, especially where those effects may be widespread, long-lasting or severe". LC 36/16, Annex 5, 1, Guidance for Consideration of Marine Geoengineering Activities, Section 2, para. 2. Geoengineering includes a wide variety of techniques, which involve either adding substances to the ocean or placing structures into the ocean, primarily for climate mitigation purposes but also for the purpose of enhancing fisheries. *Proceedings of the 2015 Science Day Symposium on Marine Geoengineering*, held on 23 April 2015 at IMO Headquarters, London, United Kingdom.

194   Resolution LC-LP.1(2008) on the Regulation of Ocean Fertilization, para. 3.

195   Resolution LC-LP.1(2008) on the Regulation of Ocean Fertilization, para. 3.

196   Resolution LC-LP.1(2008) on the Regulation of Ocean Fertilization, para. 8. The text continues: "To this end, such other activities should be considered as contrary to the aims of the Convention and Protocol and not currently qualify for any exemption from the definition of dumping in Article III.1(b) of the Convention and Article 1.4.2 of the Protocol". Even if the resolution is non-binding as such, it can be seen as a subsequent agreement or practice between the parties under the Vienna Convention, Art. 31(3) and, through that, have implications for the interpretation of the London Convention and Protocol.

COMBATTING EUTROPHICATION IN THE BALTIC SEA

to gain more knowledge about ocean fertilization, an assessment framework should be adopted in order to define projects for research purposes. That framework was to include, *inter alia*, tools for determining whether or not the proposed activity is contrary to the aims of the Convention and Protocol,[197] hence, cultivating a new way to respect and operationalize the precautionary principle, while still providing a pathway to promote further knowledge through scientific research. As a result, the contracting parties adopted a new resolution in 2010, known as the "Assessment Framework for Scientific Research Involving Ocean Fertilization",[198] which guides the parties on how to assess proposals they receive for ocean fertilization research and provides criteria for an initial assessment of such proposals.[199]

A process aimed at strengthening the legal basis for the policy on ocean fertilization, and to extend it to other forms of marine geoengineering measures,[200] reached a milestone in 2013 when the parties to the London Protocol adopted a resolution on the "Amendment to the London Protocol to regulate the placement of matter for ocean fertilization and other marine geoengineering activities".[201] The amendment adds a new Article 6bis to the Protocol which provides that "Contracting Parties shall not allow the placement of matter into the sea from vessels, aircraft, platforms or other man-made structures at sea for marine geoengineering activities listed in Annex 4, unless the listing provides that the activity or the sub-category of an activity may be authorized under a permit."

'Marine geoengineering' is defined in a new Article 1(5bis) to mean "a deliberate intervention in the marine environment to manipulate natural processes, including to counteract anthropogenic climate change and/or its impacts, and that has the potential to result in deleterious effects, especially where those effects may be widespread, long lasting and severe."

So far, Annex 4 of the London Protocol, addressed in the new article on marine geoengineering, only lists ocean fertilization. Moreover, the annex provides that ocean fertilization activities other than those listed shall not be permitted. So far, hence, ocean fertilization activities may only be considered

---

197 Resolution LC-LP.1(2008) on the Regulation of Ocean Fertilization, para. 5.

198 Resolution LC-LP.2(2010).

199 *Proceedings of the 2015 Science Day Symposium on Marine Geoengineering*, held on 23 April 2015 at IMO Headquarters, London, United Kingdom.

200 For the range of activities involved, see GESAMP, *High level review of a wide range of proposed marine geoengineering techniques*, Working Group 41, Report of 29 March 2019, available at www.gesamp.org/publications/high-level-review-of-a-wide-range-of-proposed -marine-geoengineering-techniques (accessed 2.5.2019).

201 LP.4(8), see circular LC-LP.1/Circ.61.

for a permit if they are assessed as constituting legitimate scientific research, taking into account any specific placement assessment framework. A new Annex 5 also adds the "Assessment Framework for matter that may be considered for placement under Annex 4". The Assessment Framework lists a number of points to be described, following an initial assessment of whether the activity falls within the definition of dumping at all and hence can be considered within the framework.[202]

Finally, it is important to note that if a project is accepted under the Assessment Framework, it is also to establish a thorough monitoring mechanism which takes into account both the long-term and short-term impacts of the activity. This forms a safeguard for the general lack of knowledge that remains, despite the review process, and bridges the risks that cannot be accounted for due to the fact that these are methods still under research.

As mentioned, this procedure set up under the London Dumping regime shows clear parallels with the categories of sea-based measures debated as solutions to the Baltic Sea eutrophication. As noted previously, chemical treatment of the seabed is the only measure that may meet the criterion of the definition of dumping under the London Dumping regime, depending on the substances used and the relation to the purposes of the convention. Other activities are more difficult to cover under this regime, even if they are covered by the geoengineering definition. Hence, even if the 2013 amendments were in force, the geoengineering prohibition in Article 6bis would not apply to the current cases, as long as the activity is not specifically listed in Annex 4. In addition, it should be remembered that an integral part of the definition of geoengineering measures is the potential to cause deleterious effects. On the other hand, states parties to the London Protocol hold significant discretion when deciding on the inclusion of further geoengineering measures into Annex 4 in the future. In particular, states are not, it seems, limited to activities defined as dumping or disposal in this respect. It could well be, therefore, that all categories of sea-based measures discussed here could be covered by this regime in the future, should they be included in Annex 4, which is essentially a political decision. If so, the measures could only be adopted for research purposes and only under the assessment framework set out in Annex 5 or other specific requirements accepted for the measures in question.

---

202   An arrangement of such experts in the consultation process has been adopted by the governing bodies in 2014 as annex 4 of document LC 36/16.

COMBATTING EUTROPHICATION IN THE BALTIC SEA 63

While the 2013 amendment is not formally in force, even for Finland, which is one of only three states that has ratified it,[203] it provides an interesting model for the operationalization of the precautionary principle for activities aimed at environmental protection and which entail uncertain risks. It may, therefore, also serve as a model for addressing sea-based measures more generally in a specific Baltic Sea context with the view of gaining more knowledge about the effects of such measures.[204] This is particularly relevant in view of the 2018 HELCOM Ministerial Declaration which appears to accept a certain responsibility for HELCOM to address these measures at a regional level.[205]

3.4 *Summary*

The different categories of sea-based measures give rise to rather similar questions. It has been concluded above that most of them should probably be considered to fall within the definition of 'pollution of the marine environment', but none of the categories of measures can be ruled out. Dumping, which covers some forms of seabed treatment, is the only category of measures that is clearly subject to a specific category of rules. The main rule is that it is prohibited, except where the material used is permitted under Annex I of the London Protocol. However, if dumping is done for purposes other than to discard the matter in question, there are exemptions available at all levels of law. Exemptions apply if there is sufficient environmental data and scientific evidence to support that such treatment is not "liable to create hazards to human health, to harm living resources and marine life", or that it does not go against the objectives of the relevant conventions. Even with the reasonably clear legal framework for chemical measures, in other words, the matter eventually depends on the impact of the measure.

To deal with the scientific uncertainties, the London Protocol regime has set up a strict framework for geoengineering measures, which can serve as an example for how to deal with the sea-based measures in the Baltic Sea. The assessment framework under the London Protocol is not in force yet, but once

---

203   It should be noted that the acceptance of the amendment by Finland and other states is not void of legal significance even if it is not in force. Under Art. 18(b) of the Vienna Convention, a state that has expressed its consent to be bound by a treaty is "obliged to refrain from acts which would defeat (its) object and purpose", pending its entry into force "provided that such entry into force is not unduly delayed."

204   See also Art. 24(1) of the Helsinki Convention, providing: "In order to facilitate research and monitoring activities in the Baltic Sea Area the Contracting Parties undertake to harmonize their policies with respect to permission procedures for conducting such activities."

205   See Part 5 below.

it is, the only option for implementing geoengineering measures lawfully would be solely for research purposes and with a special permit. Whether chemical treatment of the seabed would fall within the scope of this regime in the first place would, again, depend on the environmental effects, notably on whether the measure "has the potential to result in deleterious effects, especially where those effects may be widespread, long-lasting or severe."[206]

Dredging and oxygenation are subject to less specific rules. Both categories are, at an international level, regulated by general principles and overarching legislation. Given its more long-term status, oxygenation raises certain law of the sea questions, e.g. with respect to the obligation to pay due regard to the interest of other users of the sea, including safety and navigation, and questions related to the installation itself. While oxygenation could fall within the definition of geoengineering adopted under the London Protocol, it does not – in the absence of any addition of substance or "matter" into the sea – constitute dumping and would therefore not be covered by the London Protocol.

Common for all three categories of measures is that they have to be in line with a range of other more generic environmental requirements. Most of these requirements are focused on environmental assessments, procedural rules, and environmental objectives. Under EU law, the WFD, with its goal of good ecological status, introduces the most specific limitations. Since the *Weser* Judgment, space for operators to undertake measures that could have even a slightly (and perhaps temporary) deteriorating effect on the water status appears to be ruled out, unless a derogation is in place, which in turn requires its own assessments and procedures.

The Helsinki Convention places a range of relevant obligations on its states parties, but also provides significant discretion for states to make decisions on an individual case basis. Measures are to be "relevant and appropriate" for protecting the Baltic Sea. In other words, these measures have to be compared to what other mechanisms are available to achieve the same results and how they compare in terms of effectiveness, price, and environmental risk. In combination with the ecosystem approach, this includes putting it into the context of a more holistic perspective of the marine ecosystem as a whole, and the risks that these measures could pose to the ecosystem. This consideration also highlights the importance of having information about existing alternative methods available and, again, the necessity to assess whether the level of scientific knowledge is sufficient for concluding on the appropriateness of sea-based measures, both in terms of technology and in the overall ecological context.

---

206   London Protocol, Art. 1(10).

The duties to protect and preserve the marine environment, as well as the duty to take preventive measures and apply the precautionary principle, are all related to the risk and scientific uncertainties connected to sea-based measures and will inevitably play a role in that assessment. In each individual case, the environmental assessments and the extent of any scientific evidence will be crucial for the permissibility of the activity. There is little legal material to draw upon for evaluating the significance of the potential environmental benefits of the measure in the overall balancing, but on this matter, scientific evidence is even harder to obtain. Some scattered examples referred to above suggest that the long-term purpose of the measure may not be as relevant a consideration as the adverse environmental impact of the measure. At the same time, the environmental risks of not undertaking sea-based measures should be included in the equation. Here, too, however, scientific opinion diverges and the very need for such measures is doubted by several senior scientists in the region.

The main legal (and policy) limitation stemming from the sea-based measures discussed in this study is, accordingly, the lack of knowledge and certainty surrounding their short-term and long-term effects. The primary way to obtain such knowledge is through further research and tests. When faced with a similar dilemma of environmental risk, alongside the need for more knowledge in the context of ocean fertilization, the London Dumping regime developed an assessment framework to allow further activities. However, the assessment framework exercises strict control over both the purpose of the research and the activities undertaken. This could be a path forward also in relation to the sea-based measures in the Baltic Sea, and it may even be argued that some of the legal principles discussed in this section actually call for the development of a corresponding framework to advance the matter, in terms of law and otherwise.

4 The Relevance and Role of National Law

4.1 *Two Examples of National Legislation: Finland and Sweden*

In the absence of specific regulation for sea-based measures at an international level, it will largely fall upon national legislation and authorities to implement and interpret the principles in practice. It is expected that all types of sea-based measures discussed in this study will require some form of permit, for any sea area concerned, in the Baltic Sea. National legislation, on substance as well as procedure, will, therefore, play an important role in establishing the legal framework for sea-based measures. In this Part, the relevant legislation for sea-based measures of two Baltic Sea countries, Finland and Sweden, will be reviewed, emphasizing the procedural requirements and guidance on the balancing of interests. Of particular importance are the 2011 Finnish Water Act[207] and the 2014 Environmental Protection Act (EPA),[208] as well as the 1998 Swedish Environmental Code.[209]

While the relevant international and regional rules are implemented a bit differently in Sweden and Finland in terms of structure, there are not many substantive differences. Marine environmental protection legislation in both countries is heavily influenced by – and based on – international law, the Helsinki Convention, and relevant EU directives.

States have an international obligation to give effect to international rules and principles. The same applies to EU rules that are hierarchically superior to national rules. It is, therefore, both required and expected that the international and EU rules will dominate implementation at a national level. This applies irrespective of the sea area concerned, as it has been noted that the main part of the international and EU rules apply in all maritime zones, including the internal waters of the parties. The main exception to this is where national rules apply additional requirements that exceed the ones established internationally and hence impose national obligations on top of the international ones. However, on the basis of a review of the substantive rules in the two countries, there appear to be relatively few instances of such.[210]

---

207 Act 587/2011.

208 Act 527/2014. Apart from these two acts, the Act on the Protection of the Marine Environment (1415/1994) applies to Finnish vessels or individuals operating outside of the Finnish territorial sea and EEZ and other marine protection outside the EEZ; while the Act on the Organisation of River Basin Management and the Marine Strategy (1299/2004, below: *the Water Resource Management Act*) implements the MSFD and the WFD; and the Nature Conservation Act (1096/1996), is the key instrument implementing the EU's Habitats and Birds Directives. For more on these, see Vahanen Environment Oy and Centrum Balticum, 2018, 138–148 and 193–209. All Finnish official legislation can be found online at www.finlex.fi (accessed on 10 June 2019).

209 Act 1998:808. Lower level ordinances implementing the WFD and the MSFD are the Water Management Ordinance (2004:660) and the Ordinance on Marine Environment (2010:1341). Other Swedish laws of relevance include the Act on the Continental Shelf (1966:314) and the Act on Sweden's Exclusive Economic Zone (1992:1140). For more on these, see Vahanen Environment Oy and Centrum Balticum, 2018, 148–154 and 209–216.

210 One potentially relevant example of a difference between national and international rules can be found in the definition of dumping. On the one hand, Finnish law through Section 18(2) of the EPA prohibits in general terms all discharging of waste or other matter to be dumped or otherwise placed ("upottamis- tai muussa hylkäämistarkoituksessa") in Finnish territorial sea and the EEZ, regardless of the consequence of the action. In the absence of a reference to the objectives of the London dumping instruments, this is wider than the corresponding international rules. On the other hand, the Finnish rules are at

COMBATTING EUTROPHICATION IN THE BALTIC SEA 67

Rather, the main contribution of national laws in this area lies in the elaboration of a procedural framework for addressing the questions in individual cases. The main vehicle for implementing the standards discussed in this area are permits issued by the authorities for operators seeking to undertake sea-based measures. It will be these permits that, in reality, decide on whether or not an operator is entitled to carry out the measures in the sea area concerned and under what conditions.

4.2 *The Permit Procedure*

4.2.1 Introduction

As a starting point, it appears that all sea-based measures discussed in this study, irrespective of the sea area concerned, or even the scale and purpose of the activity, will be subject to some permit requirements. The application and interpretation of the national and international rules and principles will be undertaken at this phase, along with various additional conditions placed on the activity in question. It is also during the permit phase that the balancing of interests, as well as the short-term and long-term risks and the effects of any proposed measure, will be undertaken. In view of the crucial relevance of the permits for the future of sea-based measures, the details of those permits is discussed in more detail below, separately for Finland and Sweden, along with available guidance for the balancing of the different interests at stake.

4.2.2 The Finnish Permit System

4.2.2.1 *Environmental Permit*

The key instrument through which the Environment Protection Act operates is the integrated permit system, in which a permit is required for activities that cause a risk of pollution. The starting point of the environmental permit system is that the listed[211] activities creating a risk of environmental degradation require a permit. In addition, a permit is required for, *inter alia*, activities that may cause pollution of a water body and are not subject to a permit under

---

the same time narrower than the international rules, as they specifically refer to abandonment and offer no option of discarding for other purposes. Since the purpose of chemical treatment of the seabed is not (at least not merely) to abandon the chemicals but to fixate the phosphorus in the sediment, Section 18 of the Act should arguably be interpreted as permitting chemical treatment of the seabed. The Swedish Environmental Code, on its part, provides that the government, or such authority as it may designate, can grant an exemption if dumping can be done without hazards to health or the environment; Chapter 15, Section 29 of the Environmental Code. For more, see Vahanen Environment Oy and Centrum Balticum, 2018, 193–195.

211 Annexes 1 and 2 of EPA.

the Water Act.[212] Since all sea-based measures entail a risk of pollution of a water body, as a starting point, they require an environmental permit under the Environmental Protection Act, Section 27(2), unless a permit under the Water Act is required.

Derogations from the permit requirement for short-term activities undertaken on an experimental basis[213] are not possible if the permit is based on Section 27(2). Therefore, it does not seem likely that sea-based measures could be carried out with a mere notification of an experimental activity unless it can be made sure that there is no risk of water pollution.

The permit application must include necessary assessments and reports on the activity in question. Section 39 includes the specific requirements for the content of a permit application, for instance, the EIA and EIS in accordance with the 2017 Act on Environmental Impact Assessment Procedure.[214] At least larger-scale sea-based measures are likely to need an EIA.

In Finland, the national EIA system is, to a large extent, a copy of the requirements of the EU EIA Directive. In the Finnish system, the Act on Environmental Impact Assessment Procedure has a rather formal or procedural function.[215] The outcome of the EIA has no direct influence on the decision-making of other authorities. The permit application may, however, be modified by the applicant if they see that the EIA procedure gives a reason for that.[216]

The above does not, however, mean that the EIA process is without relevance in Finland. In defined situations when an EIA is needed, the application to a permit authority must include the EIA assessment report. It is also through the assessment procedure and in the assessment statement that the ecological risks, technical requirements, and other impacts are mapped and assessed.

The general duties, principles, and prohibitions in Chapter 2 of the Environmental Protection Act have to be applied. This chapter includes, e.g. the operators' knowledge requirement (of their activities' environmental impacts and risks), the duties to prevent, limit, and fight degradation, requirements concerning localization, and a special prohibition pertaining to the sea.[217]

According to Section 48 of the Environmental Protection Act, a permit shall be granted if the activity in question meets the requirements laid down in the

---

212   Section 27(2) of EPA.

213   Section 31 of EPA.

214   Act 252/2017.

215   See e.g. E. J. Hollo, *Legal Aspects on the Construction of a Gas Pipeline in the EEZ of Finland*, Petition Committee 29th January 2008 (Public Hearing in the European Parliament, Brussels: 2008) 3.

216   *Ibid.*, 4.

217   EPA, Chapter 2, Sections 6–11, 14–18.

Environmental Protection Act and the 2011 Waste Act.[218] This implies that the considerations of the permit authority are essentially judicial: the permit cannot be denied on grounds other than those defined by law. On the other hand, the permit cannot be granted if these conditions are lacking.[219]

Section 49 defines the conditions under which a permit can be granted. It is required that the activity, individually or together with other activities, when taking the permit regulations and the location of the activity into account, does not result in, *inter alia*: adverse effects on human health, other significant environmental pollution or risk thereof, pollution of soil or groundwater or sea outside Finnish territorial sea, or deterioration of special natural conditions; or pose a risk to water supply or any other potential use important to the public interest in the area of impact of the activity.

As the permit is most often either granted, wholly or in part, rather than dismissed, the substantive content of the permit, i.e. the permit conditions or permit regulations, are crucial.[220] Permits shall contain necessary provisions on, e.g. emissions, prevention of pollution, wastes, action to be taken in case of a disturbance, and other measures to prevent, reduce or assess pollution, the risk thereof, and adverse effects caused by it.[221]

When permit regulations are issued, the nature of the activity, the properties of the area where the impact of the activity appears, the impact of the activity on the environment as a whole, the significance of measures intended to prevent pollution of the environment as a whole, and the technical and financial feasibility of this action shall be taken into account. In addition, precautions for preventing accidents and limiting their consequences must be taken into account as needed.

The permit regulations are of key importance in permits for sea-based measures. The key question is whether the risk of pollution caused by the sea-based measures can be handled through the permit regulations, and if so, how the regulations should be formulated. Based on the ecosystem approach, the important question is whether the maintenance of the resilience of the marine ecosystem can be guaranteed through the permit regulations. Again, in order to understand how the risks for the water environment and ecosystem can be managed and removed, sufficient information about the risks themselves must be obtained.

---

218   Act 646/2011.
219   S. Borgström and T. Koivurova, *Environmental Law in Finland* (Tietosanoma, Finland: 2016) 50.
220   *Ibid.*, 51.
221   Section 52 of EPA.

During the environmental permit process, the Water Resource Management Act must also be taken into consideration. This Act, and the programs and strategies drawn up in accordance with it, shall be taken into account, *inter alia*, when considering the granting of a permit and the significance of potential environmental degradation of the environment caused by the activity.[222]

If an area is protected through the Nature Conservation Act or prioritized in the Marine Strategy for a certain purpose, this must be taken into account when granting a permit for sea-based measures. This, however, does not mean that any other activity would be strictly forbidden. However, a location in or close to a nature reserve would affect the balancing of interests in the permit phase since alterations of ecological values, natural conditions, landscape, etc. are more restricted in such areas.[223]

In addition, sea-based measures requiring a permit must not be situated contrary to a town plan and they shall not hinder the use of an area reserved for another use in a master plan or a regional plan.[224] In Finland, the maritime spatial planning process is only just beginning, yet it appears that actual area reservations will not be made in the maritime spatial plans, rather, the plans will be of a strategic and general nature.

4.2.2.2 *Permit under the Water Act*

While an environmental permit according to the Environmental Protection Act is an instrument for emission and pollution control, structural changes caused by water management projects are regulated through the water permit scheme according to the Water Act. Water resources management projects are subject to a permit if they may cause changes in the state, depth, water level or flow, shore, or aquatic environment of a water body, or the quality or quantity of groundwater, and this change results in certain effects listed in the Act, e.g. detrimental changes in the natural environment and the way it functions, or deterioration in the ecological status of a water body or groundwater body.[225]

Regardless of the consequences, a permit issued by a permit authority is always required for, e.g. closure or narrowing of certain channels, construction of a water, sewage, power or other cable under a general passageway, dredging of a water area when the quantity of dredged material exceeds 500 m^3, placing of dredged material into Finland's internal waters and territorial sea

---

222 Sections 49 and 51 of EPA.
223 See the Nature Protection Act, e.g. Sections 13–15, 17(a) and 64(a).
224 Section 12 of EPA.
225 Water Act, Chapter 3, Section 2.

for the purpose of dumping it, and removal of soil material from the bottom of a water area for a purpose other than ordinary household use.[226]

Sea-based measures could have some of the listed consequences and thus a permit under the Water Act would be needed. Additionally, an oxygenation pump might need construction of a cable under a general passageway and dredging includes removal of soil material from the bottom of a water area and could also include dredging over 500 m^3 and/or placing dredged material into the territorial sea.

According to Section 4 of Chapter 3 of the Water Act, there are three important legal thresholds under which water permits are considered. Firstly, a permit for a water resources management project will be granted if the project does not significantly violate public or private interests. Secondly, even if such a violation takes place, the benefit gained from the project towards public or private interests is considerable in comparison to the losses incurred. Thirdly, however, a permit may not be granted if the water resources management project jeopardizes public health or safety, causes considerable detrimental changes in the natural state of the environment or the aquatic environment and its functions, or causes considerable deterioration in the local living or economic conditions. Thus, a permit consideration under the Water Act depends normally on a weighing of interests. The third threshold, however, means that even if the benefits of the project outweigh the losses considerably, a permit cannot be granted.

When considering the conditions for granting a permit, a general assessment shall be made of the benefits and losses caused towards public interest by a water resources management project. Monetary value may be used in the assessment if the amount of the benefit or loss can be defined in monetary terms. Matters included in a river basin management plan and the Marine Strategy under Water Resource Management Act with respect to factors related to the state and use of waters in the area impacted by the project shall be taken into account in the assessment.[227] Also, town plans and to some extent regional and master plans shall be taken into account, and it shall be ensured that the permit does not complicate the preparation of a plan in any significant way.[228]

---

226   Water Act, Chapter 3, Section 3.
227   Water Act, Chapter 3, Section 6.
228   Water Act, Chapter 3, Section 5. See also the Supreme Administration Court case KHO 2014:41, where it was found that a dredging project would have considerably complicated the drafting of a partial master plan and, as a result, a permit under the Water Act could not be issued.

When assessing the private benefits and losses, the increase in the utility value of the property resulting from the improved productivity or usability of a land, water area or other property, and any other immediate benefits gained from implementing the project shall be taken into account as a private benefit gained from a water resources management project. The right of use or right to purchase granted to the applicant, the costs incurred from damage, the right of use that the applicant has separately agreed on with the stakeholder in order to implement the project, the costs of acquisition of areas voluntarily handed over to the applicant for a similar purpose, and other losses incurred by a party not participating in the project shall be taken into account as private losses.

It is stated in the preparatory work that the losses and benefits of a project shall primarily be assessed from a general point of view, but even monetary valuation of losses or benefits can be made if it is possible.[229] In the preparatory work, nature protection is mentioned as one possible public benefit. The aim of the assessment is to ensure that it can be adjusted according to different prevailing understandings of public benefit. In the assessment, social, health, and environmental perspectives shall have the same importance. Also in relation to sea-based measures, the costs or non-economic losses shall be assessed against the corresponding benefits from case to case.

Like the permits under the Environmental Protection Act, permits for water construction projects are more than mere consent. Normally, they include quite a number of various provisions by which the harmful impacts on public and private interests are reduced, eliminated, or compensated. According to Section 10 of Chapter 3 of the Water Act, the permit decision shall issue the necessary regulations on avoiding any nuisance resulting from the project and its implementation, landscaping and other elimination of traces of work, and measures and devices necessary to preserving the state of the water body and groundwater body. If a project subject to a permit under the Water Act causes environmental pollution in a water area or poses a threat of this,[230] the provisions laid down in the Environmental Protection Act on issuing permit regulations shall also apply when issuing the permit regulations under the Water Act.

4.2.2.3   *Implementation of the Water Framework Directive*
When the WFD was implemented in Finland (mainly) through the Water Resource Management Act, the directive was considered to be a planning instrument, with the environmental objectives as aims steering the planning, rather

---

229   HE 277/2009, "yksityiskohtaiset perustelut", Chapter 3, Section 6.
230   See Section 5 of EPA.

COMBATTING EUTROPHICATION IN THE BALTIC SEA

than binding requirements during the permit consideration phase, which is reflected in the Finnish legislation.[231] In the preparatory work, it was stated that the Water Resource Management Act does not cause direct obligations or economic impacts to the operators.[232] The *Weser* case has strengthened the role of environmental objectives and sparked a debate on whether there is a need to amend the Finnish legislation on this point.[233] Following *Weser*, the prohibition of a deviation of the state of a water body appears to be a clear permit prerequisite in the permit processes under the Water Act and the Environmental Protection Act.[234]

Therefore, Chapter 2 of the Water Resource Management Act on the state of water and the classification of the water are central. Whether the project causes the water classification to drop should be assessed in the permit procedure, and if it does, the permit cannot be granted, unless a derogation is granted. After the *Weser* case, the role of the derogations, the threshold for which seems to be, on a general level, relatively low, has become more significant.[235]

Chapter 4 of the Water Resource Management Act contains the environmental objectives in the river basin management plans. Section 23 contains provisions on derogating from the environmental objectives on the grounds of a significant new project and is substantially similar to the derogations in WFD art. 4(7). Derogating from the environmental objectives may be allowed if:

1) the project is very important with regard to public interest and promotes sustainable development, human health or public safety in a significant way;
2) all available measures have been taken to prevent harm; and
3) targeted benefits cannot be achieved by other technically and economically reasonable means that would be significantly better for the environment than modifying the body of water.

An account of the fulfilment of the conditions in Section 23 and an account of the modifications caused by the project in the body of water and its status must be presented in the river basin management plan. The derogation has

---

231 See A. Belinskij, 'Erittäin tärkeän yleisen edun edellytys EU:n ympäristöoikeudessa: Natura-alueen suojelusta ja vesienhoidon ympäristötavoitteista poikkeaminen uuden hankkeen takia' ('Overriding public interests in EU environmental law: Derogations from the protection of Natura 2000 sites and water quality standards to implement a new project'), in *Ympäristöjuridiikka* (2–3: 2018) 44 [in Finnish].

232 HE 120/2004 vp, 24.

233 See, e.g. A. Belinskij and T. Paloniitty, *Poikkeaminen vesienhoidon ympäristötavoitteista uuden hankkeen takia* (Edilex: 2015) available online: https://www.edilex.fi/artikkelit/15923.pdf (accessed 24.1.2019) [in Finnish].

234 *Ibid.*, 299.

235 See Belinskij, 2018, 62.

not been applied so far in Finland, but the conditions for derogating from the environmental objectives will, sooner or later, be subject to legal assessment, and it is possible that a large-scale sea-based measure project would need one. Possible derogations can be looked at every six years when the river basin management plans are being updated by the government. The conditions of derogation would be looked at in the same process.[236] Hence, in addition to the permit process, the possible need of a derogation from the environmental objectives in accordance with the Water Resource Management Act has to be taken into account when planning sea-based measures.

4.2.2.4 Summary

While the environmental permit according to the Environmental Protection Act is an instrument to deal with emissions and pollution control, structural changes caused by water management projects are regulated mainly through the water permit scheme under the Water Act. Hence, sea-based measures require a permit under either the Water Act or the Environmental Protection Act. If a project subject to a permit under the Water Act causes environmental pollution in a water area or poses a threat of such nature, the provisions laid down in the Environmental Protection Act on issuing permit regulations shall also apply.

When planning a sea-based measure project, in addition to a permit under either the Water Act or the Environmental Protection Act, the possible need for a derogation in accordance with the WFD and the Water Resource Management Act must also be taken into account. In addition, the Nature Conservation Act, plans by municipalities and regions, and maritime spatial planning impose restrictions on the use of sea-based measures. Some actions in the EEZ and outside of it require additional consents and/or permits.[237]

The Finnish permit procedures, summarised in Table 2 below, give some guidance for the balancing of interests, e.g. the possible adverse effects on human health, the possible pollution of the environment or the risk thereof, and other impacts to the environment are taken into consideration when granting a permit. In addition, permit consideration under the Water Act includes the evaluation and comparison of the public and private benefits versus the losses. Such a balancing act is done with the help of various reports in the permit application, the EIA and the EIS (if needed), and the permit regulations or conditions in the permit consideration.

---

236   Belinskij and Paloniitty, 2015, 293.
237   See the Act on the Finnish EEZ (1058/2004), Sections 6–7 and 8; and the Act on the Prevention of Marine Pollution (1415/1994), Sections 10–11.

COMBATTING EUTROPHICATION IN THE BALTIC SEA

TABLE 2   Permits of relevance for marine activities in Finland

Permit under the Water Act (EEZ, territorial sea, internal waters)	Water resource management projects described in Chapter 3, Sections 2 and 3, of the Act. Also extraction of soil materials in the EEZ. If environmental degradation is caused or may be caused, the Environmental Protection Act is applied when permit regulations are given.
Environmental permit (EEZ, territorial sea, internal waters)	If the project causes a risk of pollution of a water body and a permit under the Water Act is not required.
Notification on experimental activities under the Environmental Protection Act	Certain short-term experimental activities, but *not* if they entail a risk of water pollution → in that case, an environmental permit is needed.
Permit from the land-owner	If the activity is situated on other's property.
Notification to the Ministry of Trade and Industry	Marine scientific research in the EEZ.
Government consent in the EEZ	Construction and use of installations and structures that may interfere with the exercise of rights that, according to international law, are subject to Finnish jurisdiction. Also exploitation of natural resources of the seabed and its subsoil located in the EEZ.
Permit under the Act on the Protection of the Marine Environment (outside the EEZ)	Constructions beyond Finnish jurisdiction.

4.2.3   The Swedish Permit System

The primary frame for regulation of environmentally hazardous activities is found in Chapter 9 of the Environmental Code, which requires a permit for certain listed activities. Furthermore, there is a permit regime for water operations in Chapter 11 of the Environmental Code. The more specific requirements for activities that require a permit under Chapters 9 and 11 are laid down in ordinances issued under the Environmental Code – particularly the 2013 Ordinance on Environmental Assessment.[238] The activities listed there and their related operations may not commence without a permit. The permit

---

238   Ordinance SFS 2013:251.

sets out the scope of the activity concerned and must include the conditions under which the activity may be carried out.

The general rules of consideration in Chapter 2 of the Code are of fundamental importance for the Swedish permit system. They provide the basis for determining whether and, if so, under what conditions a permit can be issued. Moreover, all operations that require a permit must assess the effects of the activities in an EIA and EIS.

In addition, there are also certain activities that the government can declare as permissive before entering into the procedure of environmental assessment and the setting of conditions. This feature in the Swedish legal system, which is regulated in Chapter 17 of the Code, is called the 'Government's consideration of permissibility for certain matters', and it is limited to certain major infrastructure projects and nuclear activities, but could possibly also be applicable to the kind of projects that fall within the focus of this study.

4.2.3.1 *General Procedural Provisions for Sea-Based Measures*

Chapter 11 of the Environmental Code provides specific requirements for water operations and water structures.[239] In addition to Chapter 11, important provisions on water operations and water structures are also found in a specific law, the 1998 Law with specific rules for water operations.[240] Both dredging and the kind of installation that is connected to oxygenation are found among the specific activities regulated in Chapter 11 of the Environmental Code.[241] Dumping, however, is not. It is regulated by the waste management laws in Chapter 15 of the Environmental Code.

Water operations or structures at a larger scale, or with more significant impact for the environment and for sustainable development, could also be subject to the government's consideration of permissibility for certain matters established in Chapter 17 of the Environmental Code.[242] It is possible that a large-scale installation for oxygenation could match those criteria. If a matter is the object of such permissibility, it will still need to go through a permit procedure where the conditions of the permit will be established.

For sea-based measures taking place beyond the Swedish territorial sea, the Act on the Swedish EEZ and the Swedish Continental Shelf Act are also central, in addition to the Environmental Code. Like in Finland, exploration of the continental shelf, the investigation, extraction, and other utilization of

---

239   Swedish Environmental Code (1998:808) (Environmental Code) Chapter 11, Section 1.
240   Act (SFS 1998:812) Containing Special Provisions concerning Water Operations.
241   Environmental Code, Chapter 11, Section 3.1 and Section 3.4.
242   Environmental Code, Chapter 17, Section 3.

natural resources in the EEZ, as well as the establishment and utilization of installations and other equipment for commercial purposes in the EEZ require additional consents and licenses.[243]

There are several balancing principles provided under the Swedish legislation affecting the permissibility of sea-based measures. The regulation of water operations and water structures sets out the main criteria for their permissibility.

The main principle for water operations and water structures regulated by Chapter 11 of the Environmental Code is that such operations and structures require a permit.[244] Some exceptions from this main rule are established,[245] but they are likely to be deemed not applicable regarding sea-based measures that entail a risk of environmental degradation and are targeted towards eutrophication, which is not a temporary change.

For a water operation or water structure to be permitted, the activity or the structure must meet a number of requirements established in the Environmental Code. In particular, the requirements in the general rules of consideration provided in Chapter 2 of the Code have to be applied. This includes different forms of precautionary and preventive measures, and rather strict requirements on localization, which is an interesting matter in this context. Sea-based measures must generally be placed where the problems are apparent, but these could also be areas that are more sensitive to different forms of disturbance.

When considering the localization, the general provisions for management of land and water areas, Chapters 3 and 4 of the Environmental Code also provide a balancing tool for how the areas are to be used. These rules for management include a differentiation between different land and water areas, meaning that some areas must be prioritized or protected for different purposes.

The maritime spatial plans work in a similar way to the management plan for land and water in Chapters 3 and 4 of the Code but are more general. The plans made by municipalities in water areas in the territorial sea affect the use of those areas. Moreover, Chapters 7 and 8 of the Environmental Code contain rules on nature protection and restrict the use of the protected areas. Depending on the level of nature protection, exploitation in such areas will be restricted or even forbidden.

---

243 The Continental Shelf Law, Sections 2–3, and The Act on the Swedish EEZ, Section 5.
244 Environmental Code, Chapter 11, Section 9.
245 Environmental Code, Section 12 and Section 15 of Chapter 11.

4.2.3.2 *Permits for Hazardous Activities*

The Environmental Code also maintains other principles and rules on permits. If a water operation or water structure falls within the definition of 'environmentally hazardous activities' according to Chapter 9, Section 1 of the Code, it is regulated also by those requirements. Among the sea-based measures, a pumping installation appears to be the only one that could meet the criteria for hazardous activities, since it is the only measure that is based on a (semi-) permanent installation or structure, which thus will have an impact on the surrounding environment.

The activities that require a permit are listed in the Ordinance on Environmental Assessment.[246] In addition to this list, there is a possibility for the supervisory authority to request that an operator applies for a permit even when it is not listed, whereby it is likely to cause significant harm to the environment.[247] A pumping installation may fall under this requirement, but since it – if established in the territorial sea or internal waters – would be subject to a permit procedure according to Chapter 11 of the Code, it is likely that an authority would not require an additional double permit procedure for the operation.

4.2.3.3 *Environmental Quality Standards and the Implementation of the WFD*

Provided certain limited exceptions, permits, approvals, and exemptions cannot be granted for activities which are likely to lead to non-compliance with EQS. The permit authority may revise a permit for an activity with respect to the permissible volume of production or the scope of the activity, alter or cancel conditions or other provisions, or issue new provisions where the activity is, to a significant extent, responsible for an infringement of EQS.[248] The regulation on EQS in Chapter 5 of the Environmental Code also, to a large extent, incorporates the WFD into the Swedish law and the regulation has been changed specifically to reflect the outcome of the *Weser* judgment. Hence, for a permit procedure for sea-based measures, these rules have a significant impact since it is possible that they will have adverse effects on the EQS. The implementation of the *Weser* Judgment will further limit the possibilities to receive a permit in certain areas.

---

246 Environmental Code, Chapter 9, Section 6.
247 Environmental Code, Chapter 9, Section 6a.
248 Swedish Environmental Protection Agency (Naturvårdsverket), Report 6790, *Swedish Environmental Law – An introduction to the Swedish legal system for environmental protection*, October 2017, 19; and Environmental Code, Chapter 2, Section 7; Chapter 5; and Chapter 24.

4.2.3.4 *Summary*

Sea-based measures are regulated in Sweden mainly through Chapters 11, 15, and 9 of the Environmental Code and the related Ordinances. It also appears that they require a permit in accordance with the Swedish law, as they entail a risk of environmental degradation. Water operations or structures at a larger scale, or with a more significant impact on the environment and sustainable development, may also be the subject of the government's consideration in determining permissibility. Some actions in the EEZ and outside of it require additional consents and/or permits, as is the case in the Finnish regulatory framework.

Similar balancing principles and requirements to those provided in the Finnish legislation can also be found in the Swedish regulation. For instance, environmental degradation shall be prevented and the water operation shall be assessed from a cost-benefit analysis. Compared to Finland, the Swedish legislation contains more specific rules on the environmental quality standards in implementing the WFD and the *Weser* case.

4.3 *Conclusion on the Role of National Procedures*

The goal-orientation, the holistic and integrated understanding, as well as the ecosystem approach in international law, at both global and regional level, are reflected in the fact that sea-based measures are not specifically regulated on those levels, nor are they on the higher legal national levels. The focus is on ecological objectives and indicators, which leads to the fact that much emphasis is on the national permit procedure where the essential weighing, balancing, and technical applicability are assessed on a case-by-case basis.

Under both national legal systems, many parallel procedural rules and conditions apply. All sea-based measures contemplated here require some form of permit, irrespective of where in the Baltic Sea they are placed. In some cases, there could also be opportunities for a government or authority to consider the permissibility of activities on a case-by-case basis. If sea-based measures, mainly various forms of chemical treatment, fall within the definition of dumping, the main rule prohibits the activity. In such cases, exemptions must be granted.

Whether the matter relates to a permit, exemption, or other rules of consideration, an assessment of the potential harm to the environment is the key to the level of control and conditions for any such measures to be accepted. Hence, at a national level, too, knowledge of such effects is crucial for the legal assessment. A key instrument here then, in Sweden as well as in Finland, is the EIA, through which the different (potential) risks, benefits, and other interests or issues are to be presented and assessed. This information and any knowledge gaps it may highlight is of critical importance when deciding on the permit and the permit regulations/conditions.

From an ecosystem point of view, the resilience of the marine ecosystem should not be reduced, from either a long-term or short-term perspective. However, there is no available legal practice for cases comparable to sea-based measures involving a risk of temporarily weakening the state of the sea through a measure that, in the long-term, seeks to improve its state. The regulations or conditions linked with the permit are significant for managing the risk of environmental degradation. It is for the operator of the measure to demonstrate that it has sufficient information about the risks in order to be able to manage them adequately.

Meeting the various requirements and assessments linked to the permit procedure accordingly presupposes significant knowledge about the environment, the technical process, and the wider environmental impact of the measure. While the lack of such information constitutes an obstacle to a full legal review, it also emphasizes the quest for further research, also at a national level. Small-scaled sea-based measure projects have already been given permits and have taken place in both Sweden and Finland, and some lessons can no doubt be learned from them.[249]

On the other hand, in both countries, water resource management projects require a permit where a general assessment shall be made of the benefits and losses caused to public and private interest. In this assessment, values other than environmental values must also be assessed. In Finland, a permit for a water resources management project will be granted if the project does not significantly violate public or private interests. Even whereby such a violation takes place, a permit may still be granted if the benefit gained from the project towards public or private interests is considerable in comparison to the losses incurred. However, if the water resources management project jeopardizes public health or safety, causes considerable detrimental changes in the natural state of the environment or the aquatic environment and its functions, or causes considerable deterioration in the local living or economic conditions, a permit cannot be granted despite the weighing of the public and private interests and losses.

The various provisions, particularly those in the Finnish Environmental Protection Act and the Swedish Environmental Code, respectively, provide other balancing principles. Such a balancing act may be based on different conditions. One way this may be conducted is so that there is a direct balancing

---

249   See, e.g. Vahanen Environment Oy and Centrum Balticum, 2018, 55; Rantajärvi et al., 2012; and Stigebrandt et al., 2015a.

COMBATTING EUTROPHICATION IN THE BALTIC SEA

of interests (land/water use), whereby the interest that is most in line with a sustainability perspective prevails. Another possible outcome – probably the most common – is that the balancing results in a sufficient amount of preventive measures so that the activity or operation planned for (the land/water use) is not in conflict with other interests and that the protected area will not be harmed.

Since the national permit procedure is the phase at which the environmental risks are eventually estimated and weighed against other effects of sea-based measures, it is potentially very important in filling the voids and imperfections of applicable international and regional rules. However, national rules, at least in Finland and Sweden, do not add much in terms of specific regulation of sea-based measures. The legislation in both countries offers some guidance for how the balancing should be conducted, and the tools and criteria that should be used, however, the permit decisions and the balancing are case specific. The national regulation reflects the fact that the permit processes have not been designed for projects that aim at the (usually long-term) improvement of the environmental state but entail a risk of (at least) short-term environmental degradation.

In view of this uncertainty, and the obvious risk for diverging national policies that it entails, it seems clear that more precise guidance would be needed to assist national or regional authorities and to achieve regional policy consistency. The first steps towards adopting a region-wide policy for sea-based measures have recently been undertaken at HELCOM.

5   Recent Development at HELCOM

Traditionally, HELCOM's policy on eutrophication has been focused on land-based measures.[250] The position has been that reducing pollution at the source is the only way of achieving the aim of a Baltic Sea unaffected by eutrophication and maintaining a good environmental status in the long-term.[251] More recently, HELCOM has indicated more openness towards sea-based measures. In March 2018, nutrient reserves and technical sea-based measures were addressed for the first time in a HELCOM Ministerial Declaration, highlighting

---

250   See, e.g. the HELCOM action areas: http://www.helcom.fi/action-areas (accessed 24.1.2019).

251   See, e.g. HELCOM Copenhagen Ministerial Declaration, *Taking Further Action to Implement the Baltic Sea Action Plan – Reaching Good Environmental Status for a healthy Baltic Sea*, Copenhagen, Denmark, 3 October 2013.

it as an important part of future work to reduce eutrophication in the Baltic Sea.[252] Para. 26 of the 2018 Ministerial Declaration reads as follows:

> We encourage ... undertaking research on the potential of measures to manage internal nutrient reserves that have accumulated in the sediments due to anthropogenic activities in the last decades; We emphasize that the risks to ecosystem and human health stemming from measures to manage internal nutrient reserves, as well as the long-term sustainability of their effects, need to be considered and thoroughly evaluated; We also encourage in parallel developing and applying a risk assessment framework in HELCOM to meet the necessary environmental requirements for measures planned for the open sea and any other measures having potentially significant transboundary effects; We also acknowledge the need to elaborate in line with the Helsinki Convention commonly agreed regional principles as guidance for internal nutrient reserves management.

Since then, the HELCOM Pressure working group has agreed on updated Terms of Reference for the drafting of 'regional principles for risk assessment framework for management of internal nutrient reserves'.[253] These Terms of Reference were also approved by the Heads of Delegations (HOD) at their meeting in December 2018.[254] The working group agreed to prepare a draft for a risk assessment framework and for regional principles as guidance for nutrient reserves management. This should, among other things, cover: scale and location of the measures; scientific research and deployment; coverage in terms of internal nutrient management measures; regional principles guiding the management of internal nutrient reserves; and the risk assessment framework. A decision was also taken by the HOD to develop a first draft of the risk assessment framework and the regional principles.[255]

The developments in HELCOM suggest that the focus of the activities to curb eutrophication in the Baltic Sea is no longer limited to land-based measures. Despite the hesitation of certain HELCOM states, there is now an opening for the inclusion of sea-based measures among the mitigation measures. In a recent survey of certain key stakeholders in the Baltic Sea region,

---

252 HELCOM Ministerial Declaration, Brussels, March 2018, paras. 24–26.

253 HELCOM Pressure 9-2018, paras. 6.10–12.

254 Outcome of HELCOM HOD 55-2018, para. 4.31. See also at paras. 3.15–17, where an alternative structure for updating pressures under the BSAP, separating between land-based and sea-based pressures, was discussed and partially endorsed.

255 HELCOM HOD 55-2018, Document 4–8.

COMBATTING EUTROPHICATION IN THE BALTIC SEA 83

this development seems to have found support. The general view among the respondents was that HELCOM should play a major role in the development of policy and rules for sea-based measures.[256] As the interest in sea-based measures increases, a common strategy with common solutions for how to proceed and handle the risks will eventually become necessary. The proposed risk assessment framework and regional principles are valuable tools for guiding the national authorities and for preventing divergent applications of sea-based measures in the Baltic Sea. Even in a non-binding format, the HELCOM risk assessment framework would serve to clarify the legal picture for national authorities.

On the basis of the legal review undertaken here, some substantive elements seem particularly relevant to include in the future work conducted by HELCOM in relation to the matter. As long as the environmental risks are not well understood, environmental laws are difficult to apply even where legal rules and principles are available and applicable. For the same reason, it is difficult to outline how the balance of risks should be struck in the abstract. For these reasons, it would seem particularly relevant to provide guidance on the application and interpretation of the precautionary principle in the context of sea-based measures. This principle will have a key impact on how authorities will decide on proposed activities in their sea areas. In view of the scientific uncertainty and the hesitancy exhibited by the broad range of actors in the development of sea-based measures in the Baltic Sea, it would further seem justified to limit the application to research operations, at least until more information is obtained. This would correspond to the precautionary approach taken towards marine geoengineering measures in the London Dumping framework. Whether or to what extent commercial operations should also be allowed needs to be clarified in the framework. Independently of the decisions made in this regard, it seems necessary to further explore and clarify the risks and benefits linked to different kinds of sea-based measures – both in terms of direct effects and at the level of the ecosystem as a whole. The first step towards a workable legal framework for the Baltic Sea is the acknowledgement

---

256 See Vahanen Environment Oy and Centrum Balticum, 2018, 156–157. Some of the respondents called for special regulation on sea-based measures at national, international, and HELCOM level, perhaps even through the establishment of a new division of HELCOM with more regulatory and legal authority. Common procedures, processes, and guidance were also called for. The permit practices should be coherent and the potential problems must be thought through. If sea-based measures were to be undertaken at a large-scale, the involvement of regional authorities (HELCOM) and scientific institutions was considered to be particularly important. Close coordination with the EU was also considered to be important in this respect.

of the need to address the matter at a regional level. In this sense, the recent initiatives conducted within HELCOM represent a very welcome first step.

6 Concluding Observations

6.1 *On the Legal Position of Sea-Based Measures*

Sea-based measures represent a relatively new development and there are no laws relating specifically to such measures. This study has reviewed what laws and principles apply to different types of measures in different sea areas. The relevant rules and principles are mainly those that govern different forms of marine activities and acts which may result in potential effects on the marine environment. A broad range of such rules and principles apply, at different levels of regulation. The main material rules originate from international and EU legislation, while implementation takes place at a national level.

In the end, the legality of any kind of sea-based measure, in any sea area, depends on the risks they present – in the short and long-term – balanced against their long-term benefits. In view of this, a particular category of measures cannot be legally preferred over another without having regard to their performance and environmental impact. If a particular measure improves the marine environment without much risk, it is legally easy to justify, while, conversely, a measure with uncertain benefits and large risks meets resistance in a variety of applicable legal rules and principles across many levels.

A problem with sea-based measures is that their potential impact in this regard is disputed and not well understood. There is no certainty or consensus among scientists as to what the likely environmental outcome of the sea-based measures will be, in particular for large-scale measures. This, in turn, highlights the need for more knowledge and the availability of a proper national procedure for evaluating the proposed measures based on the best available scientific knowledge.

Another problem for establishing the legal rights and obligations that apply to sea-based measures is that many of the key environmental obligations and principles involved could work both ways, in view of the common concern that underlies both the arguments in favour of such measures and the ones against them. A duty to protect the marine environment, for example, could be interpreted as a duty to take such measures and a duty to abstain from them, depending on their effect, which leads back to the scientific uncertainty.

In practice, the balancing of interests will take place at a national level during the permit process. This process will, therefore, be where the relevant rules and standards are implemented most concretely, on a case-by-case basis.

COMBATTING EUTROPHICATION IN THE BALTIC SEA

In this process, the permit regulations, in the form of implementing obligations and conditions, are of crucial relevance. Any kind of sea-based measure is subject to a permit, at least in Finland and Sweden, and this will accordingly be the procedural framework in which short-term and long-term risks and benefits will be weighed against each other, on the basis of applicable law. This law includes principles to deal with scientific uncertainty, notably in the form of the precautionary principle, but not even that principle can be applied without regard to the facts and information available in the individual case.

6.2 Observations Relating to Regulatory Voids

A review of the legal status of sea-based measures also serves as a study of how environmental law functions when 'left on its own', without assistance from rules targeting the precise subject area in question. Based on this survey, the answer seems to be, not very well. However, this is in large part due to factors that go beyond the law. The uncertain legal status of sea-based measures has more to do with doubts surrounding the environmental effects of sea-based measures than with the ambiguities in the law as such.

It is clear that the absence of specific rules on the topic signifies that a very large number of legal rules and principles apply to the subject matter. On the other hand, it also signifies that the rules that do apply tend to be the rules and principles of environmental law which are formulated at a high level of generality and tend to be of limited assistance for resolving any particular question at hand. At this level of generality, the rules provide little more guidance than emphasizing that if a given activity has positive environmental effects, it is lawful, and if it causes environmental harm, it is not. These rules and principles are set up to deal with a scenario where environmental interests compete with other societal interests, but even in that scenario, there are few established principles on how different interests should be balanced against each other.

In the case of sea-based measures, an additional challenge is that both the risks and benefits of the measures relate to concerns about the marine environment. An additional question is therefore whether the long-term environmental objectives of the measure could serve to justify short-term harm. Key principles such as the no-harm principle, the ecosystem approach, and the obligation to protect the marine environment could easily work both ways in this situation, and neither law, "hard" or "soft", nor existing international practice offer much guidance with respect to the balancing between short-term and long-term effects.

Environmental principles generally focus on protection and prevention from environmental harm and their application presumes that some amount of information is available about technologies, risks, and consequences. In the case of sea-based measures, this is not generally the case, which drains the legal rules and principles of their substantive content. This invokes the critical question as to how the law deals with scientific uncertainty.

The one principle specifically developed to deal with scientific uncertainty in an environmental context is the precautionary principle. However, this principle is not as recognized as many other environmental principles as to its legal status and, even if it were, its substantive scope and normative implications are subject to widely differing interpretations. In a Baltic Sea context, such concerns are alleviated by the presence of a fairly strictly worded precautionary principle in the Helsinki Convention, but even if sea-based measures were deemed to meet the criteria for triggering its application, the question of what the prescribed "preventive measures" should consist of would still be left open. In view of the convergence of concerns, both the approval and the rejection of a proposed measure could be considered to be an act of prevention.

The ambiguity of international law in this field leaves more space for other regulatory layers to assume a role. In the present context, the role of EU law turns out to be particularly significant. It is EU law that places the clearest – and tightest – limitations on what measures can be approved for eight of the nine littoral states surrounding the Baltic Sea. The most direct limitations for authorities to approve projects that entail environmental degradation does not necessarily follow from EU legislation as such. However, it has been laid down in subsequent interpretations of the legislation in certain landmark judgments by the CJEU on how the permits under the Water Framework Directive should be approached by member state authorities.

The significance attributed to the water quality requirements of the WFD has also had the consequence that the most important spatial limit for sea-based measures presently is one without any basis in the law of the sea. Given that the ruling in the *Weser* case is limited to the WFD, and cannot easily be extended to the MSFD, it is the 1 nm limit from the baseline of the WFD that presently constitutes the most important dividing line between flexibility and rigidity. While EU member states have large flexibility to approve measures beyond this limit, activities that cause degradation of a single environmental quality element cannot be approved within this limit, unless they are specifically foreseen and exempted under the Directive. This highlights the role of derogations under Article 4(7) of the WFD, but it is not obvious that sea-based measures would qualify under the conditions for derogations listed in that paragraph.

The procedural framework for implementing the international and EU rules operates at a national level. Sea-based measures discussed in this study will supposedly require a national permit in all Baltic Sea states, and it will be public authorities (government, regional, or local authority, depending on the location and nature of the operation) who will eventually decide on the permit, and place the conditions for the operation of the measures in their waters. Through a number of procedural safeguards at a national level, it can be ensured that the operator of the measure supplies the best available information about its impact, and assumes responsibility for the operation.

However, the procedural rules do not offer much additional substantive guidance for authorities. The lack of substantive guidance on how the different interests involved should be balanced against each other, in combination with the significant flexibility that is offered to individual states by international and EU rules, in particular beyond the 1 nm limit, opens up for diverging policies in the Baltic Sea.

6.3   *On the Way Ahead*

If the interest in sea-based measures to fight eutrophication in the Baltic Sea continues to grow, as seems to be the case, a common Baltic-Sea-wide coordination of the coastal states' policies on the matter would seem legally justifiable and even necessary. Apart from streamlining the national policies within the region on a subject matter of common regional concern, regional principles would also contribute to the transparency of the measures and their effects, which seems crucial from all perspectives, including for clarifying the rights and duties involved.

Even regional guidance of a purely recommendatory nature could provide important support for national authorities in charge of assessing permit applications. A more solid legal construction, in the form of an amended annex to the Helsinki Convention, would, through the EU's participation in the Helsinki Convention, give priority to the annex over any conflicting EU directives or regulations.

Such common principles could ideally be applied with respect to any sea-based measure, irrespective of their location and size. The principles could include guidance on matters, such as the purpose, location, and methodologies of the activity, information needed for issuing a permit, assessment of risks, monitoring of progress, and on sharing the information of the results. In addition, the principles or guidelines could address policy issues on which there is currently legal uncertainty, such as whether (local or remote) mitigation measures (ecological compensation) could be accepted as a tool of compensation for the environmental harm caused by sea-based measures.

As has been noted repeatedly in this study, a key feature of sea-based measures is the scientific uncertainty that surrounds the technical potential of such measures and their short-term and long-term impact on the marine environment. In view of this, and of the precautionary principle as laid down in Article 3(2) of the Helsinki Convention, it seems justified for public authorities to prioritize measures aimed at learning more about such measures, before paving the way for the implementation of large-scale facilities involving uncertain risks. To put it differently, it seems difficult at this stage to justify the approval of sea-based measures other than for research purposes with high demands on the transparency of the methods and results.

The model developed for marine geoengineering measures in the London Dumping framework in 2013, which also conditions approval on scientific research, could provide a useful blueprint for HELCOM's further work in this area. However, merely copying that framework is hardly an option, in view of the many features that distinguish sea-based measures from other marine geoengineering measures. Several unique features of sea-based measures call for tailor-made provisions, starting from the very definition of sea-based measures. Other particularities, such as the complexity of assessing the risks and benefits, the role of coastal states that follows from the absence of areas beyond national jurisdiction in the Baltic Sea, and issues linked to the convergence of concerns between the purpose of the measures and the risk that they present, would similarly call for a separate regional regime for sea-based measures in the Baltic Sea and beyond. For large-scale research in this field, it may even be justifiable to coordinate the research itself, and the permit processes, at a Baltic Sea regional level. In view of the many environmental, political, and legal uncertainties linked to sea-based measures, the speedy implementation of common research projects in this area would be a very welcome development.

List of References

Bibliography

Belinskij, A., 'Erittäin tärkeän yleisen edun edellytys EU:n ympäristöoikeudessa: Natura-alueen suojelusta ja vesienhoidon ympäristötavoitteista poikkeaminen uuden hankkeen takia' ('Overriding public interests in EU environmental law: Derogations from the protection of Natura 2000 sites and water quality standards to implement a new project'), in *Ympäristöjuridiikka* (2–3: 2018) [in Finnish].

Belinskij, A. and Paloniitty, T., *Poikkeaminen vesienhoidon ympäristötavoitteista uuden hankkeen takia* (Edilex: 2015) available online: https://www.edilex.fi/artikkelit/ 15923.pdf (accessed on 24 January 2019).

Birnie, P., Boyle, A., and Redgwell, C., *International Law and the Environment*, 3rd ed. (Oxford University Press, New York: 2009).

Borgström, S. and Koivurova, T., *Environmental Law in Finland* (Tietosanoma, Finland: 2016).

Elmgren, R., 'Understanding Human Impact on the Baltic Ecosystem: Changing Views in Recent Decades' in *Man and the Baltic Sea* (Ambio, Vol. 30, No. 4/5: 2001) 222–231.

Franckx, E., 'Gaps in Baltic Sea Maritime Boundaries', in H. Ringbom (ed.), *Regulatory Gaps in Baltic Sea Governance – Selected Issues* (Springer: 2018).

Galaz, V., 'Geo-engineering, governance, and social-ecological systems: critical issues and joint research needs', in *Ecology and Society* (vol. 17, no. 1: 2012) http://dx.doi.org/10.5751/ES-04677-170124.

Güssow K. et al., 'Ocean iron fertilization: Why further research is needed', in *Marine Policy* (vol. 34, no. 5: 2010) 911–918.

Gustafsson, B. G., et al., *Reconstructing the Development of Baltic Sea Eutrophication 1850–2006* (Ambio, Vol. 41: 2013).

Langlet, D. and Mahmoudi, S., *EU Environmental Law and Policy* (Oxford University Press, Oxford: 2016).

Larsson, U., Elmgren, R., and Wulff, F., *Eutrophication and the Baltic Sea: Causes and Consequences* (Ambio, Vol. 14, No. 1: 1985).

Newcombe, G. et al., *Management Strategies for Cyanobacteria (Blue-Green Algae): A Guide for Water Utilities* (Research Report No 74, CRF for Water Quality and Treatment: 2010).

Nilsson, A. K. and Bohman, B., 'Legal prerequisites for ecosystem-based management in the Baltic Sea area: The example of eutrophication', in *Ambio* (vol. 44, sup. 3: 2015).

Paloniitty, T., 'Analysis: The Weser Case: Case C-461/13 BUND V GERMANY', in *Journal of Environmental Law* (vol. 28, no. 1: 2016) 151–158, doi: 10.1093/jel/eqv032.

Rantajärvi, E. (ed.) et.al., *Controlling benthic release of phosphorus in different Baltic Sea scales. Final Report on the result of the PROPPEN Project (802-0301-08) to the Swedish Environmental Protection Agency, Formas and VINNOVA* (Finnish Environmental Institute: 2012). Available online: http://hdl.handle.net/10138/167975 (accessed on 15 January 2018).

van Rijswick, H. F. M. W. and Backes, C. W., "Ground Breaking Landmark Case on Environmental Quality Standards?: The Consequences of the CJEU '*Weser*-judgment' (C-461/13) for Water Policy and Law and Quality Standards in EU Environmental Law", in *Journal for European Environmental & Planning Law* (vol. 12: 2015) 363–377.

Roach, J. A., 'Today's Customary Law of the Sea', in *Ocean Development & International Law* (45, 3: 2014).

Rothwell, D. R. and Stephens, T., *The International Law of the Sea*, Second ed. (Hart Publishing, Oxford/Portland: 2016).

Rydin, E. et al., 'Remediation of a Eutrophic Bay in the Baltic Sea', in *Environmental Science and Technology* (vol. 51, no. 8: 2017).

Sands, P. and Peel, J., *Principles of International Environmental Law*, 3rd ed. (Cambridge University Press, Cambridge: 2012).

Sarvilinna A. and Sammalkorpi, I., *Rehevöityneen järven kunnostus ja hoito* (*Restoration and management of eutrophic lakes*) (Environment Guide, Finnish Environment Institute: 2010).

Scott, K. N., 'Geoengineering and the Marine Environment', in Rosemary Rayfuse (ed.), *Research Handbook on International Marine Environmental Law* (Edward Elgar Publishing, Cheltenham: 2015).

Söderasp, J., Law in Integrated and Adaptive Governance of Freshwaters: A Study of the Swedish Implementation of the EU Water Framework Directive, Doctoral Thesis (Luleå University of Technology, Luleå: 2018).

Stigebrandt, A., 'On the response of the Baltic Proper to changes of the total phosphorus supply', in *Ambio* (vol. 47: 2018) 31–44. doi: 10.1007/s13280-017-0933-7.

Stigebrandt, A. and O. Kalén, 'Improving oxygen conditions in the deeper parts of the Bornholm Sea by pumped injection of winter water', in *Ambio* (vol. 42, no. 5: 2013) 587–595. doi: 10.1007/s13280-012-0356-4.

Stigebrandt, A., R. Rosenberg, L. Råman-Vinnå, and M. Ödalen, 'Consequences of artificial deepwater ventilation in the Bornholm Basin for oxygen conditions, cod reproduction and benthic biomass – A model study', in *Ocean Science* (vol. 11: 2015a) 93–110. doi: 10.5194/os-11-1-2015.

Stigebrandt, A., L. Rahm, L. Viktorsson, M. Ödalen, P. O. J. Hall, and B. Liljebladh, 'A new phosphorus paradigm for the Baltic Proper', in *Ambio* (vol. 43: 2014) 634–643. doi: 10.1007/s13280-013-0441-3.

Stigebrandt, A., B. Liljebladh, L. De Brabandere, M. Forth, Å. Granmo, P. O. J. Hall, J. Hammar, D. Hansson, M. Kononets, M. Magnusson, F. Norén, L. Rahm, A. Treusch, and L. Viktorsson, 'An experiment with forced oxygenation of the deep-water of the anoxic By Fjord, western Sweden', in *Ambio* (vol. 44: 2015b) 42–54. doi: 10.1007/s13280-014-0524-9.

Tanaka, Y., *The International Law of the Sea*, Second ed. (Cambridge University Press, Cambridge: 2015).

Williamson, P. et al., 'Ocean fertilization for geoengineering: A review of effectiveness, environmental impacts and emerging governance', in *Process Safety and Environmental Protection* (vol. 90, no. 6: 2012) 475–488.

International Law

Convention on Biological Diversity (adopted 5 June 1992, entered into force 29 December 1993) 1760 UNTS 79 (the CBD).

Convention on Environmental Impact Assessment in a Transboundary Context (adopted 25 February 1991, entered into force 10 September 1997) 1989 UNTS 309 (the Espoo Convention).

COMBATTING EUTROPHICATION IN THE BALTIC SEA

Convention on the Law of the Sea (adopted 10 December 1982, entered into force 16 November 1994) 1833 UNTS 3 (UNCLOS).

Convention on the Prevention of Marine Pollution by Dumping of Wastes and Other Matter (adopted 29 December 1972, entered into force 30 August 1975) 1046 UNTS 120 (the London Convention).

Convention on the Protection of the Marine Environment of the Baltic Sea Area (adopted 9 April 1992, entered into force 17 January 2000) 2099 UNTS 195 (Helsinki Convention).

LC 36/16, Annex 5, 1, 'Guidance for Consideration of Marine Geoengineering'.

London Protocol Resolution LC-LP.1(2008) on the Regulation of Ocean Fertilization, adopted on the Thirtieth Meeting of the Contracting Parties to the London Convention and the Third Meeting of the Contracting Parties to the London Protocol.

Protocol to the Convention on the Prevention of Marine Pollution by Dumping of Wastes and Other Matter (adopted 7 November 1996, entered into force 24 March 2006) 36 ILM 1 (London Protocol).

The 1995 United Nations Agreement for the Implementation of the Provisions of the United Nations Convention on the Law of the Sea of 10 December 1982 relating to the Conservation and Management of Straddling Fish Stocks and Highly Migratory Fish Stocks (the UN Fish Stocks Agreement) 2167 UNTS 88.

The 1997 Kyoto Protocol to the United Nations Framework Convention on Climate Change (the Kyoto Protocol) 37 ILM 22(1998).

United Nations Declaration on Environment and Development (adopted 16 June 1992) 31 ILM 1992 (the Rio Declaration).

Vienna Convention on the law of treaties (adopted 23 May 1969, entered into force 27 January 1980) 1155 UNTS 331 (the Vienna Convention).

World Charter for Nature, 1982, UN General Assembly, UNGA Res. 37/7, 22 ILM 455 (1983).

EU Law

Council Directive 92/43/EEC of 21 May 1992 on the conservation of natural habitats and of wild fauna and flora (The Habitats Directive) OJ L 206/7.

Directive 2000/60/EC of the European Parliament and of the Council of 23 October 2000 establishing a framework for Community action in the field of water policy (Water Framework Directive) OJ L 327/1 (the WFD).

Directive 2008/56/EC of the European Parliament and of the Council of 17 June 2008 establishing a framework for community action in the field of marine environmental policy (Marine Strategy Framework Directive) OJ L 164/19 (the MSFD).

Directive 2008/98/EC of the European Parliament and of the Council of 19 November 2008 on waste and repealing certain Directives (Waste Framework Directive) OJ L 312/3.

Directive 2009/147/EC of the European Parliament and of the Council of 30 November 2009 on the conservation of wild birds (the Birds Directive) OJ L 20/7.

Directive 2011/92/EU of the European Parliament and of the Council of 13 December 2011 on the assessment of the effects of certain public and private projects on the environment (EIA Directive) OJ L 26/1.

Directive 2014/89/EU of the European Parliament and of the Council of 23 July 2014 establishing a framework for maritime spatial planning OJ L 257/135 (the MSPD).

The Treaty on the Functioning of the European Union OJ C 326/47 (TFEU).

HELCOM Documents

HELCOM 2017, Memo of the HELCOM-EUSBSR Workshop on internal nutrient reserves, held 28–29 November 2017 Gothenburg, Sweden.

HELCOM Baltic Sea Action Plan, (BSAP), adopted on 15 November 2007 in Krakow, Poland by the HELCOM Extraordinary Ministerial Meeting.

HELCOM Brussels Ministerial Declaration, 6 March 2018.

HELCOM Copenhagen Ministerial Declaration, *Taking Further Action to Implement the Baltic Sea Action Plan – Reaching Good Environmental Status for a healthy Baltic Sea*, Copenhagen Denmark, 3 October 2013.

HELCOM Copenhagen Ministerial Declaration, *Taking Further Action to Implement the Baltic Sea Action Plan – Reaching Good Environmental Status for a healthy Baltic Sea*, Copenhagen Denmark, 3 October 2013, including the acts adopted (HELCOM Palette of optional agro-environmental measures and Recommendations).

HELCOM Ecological Objectives for an Ecosystem Approach, document for HELCOM Stakeholder Conference on the Baltic Sea Action Plan, Helsinki, Finland, 7 March 2006.

HELCOM Guidelines for Management of Dredged Material at Sea, Adopted by HELCOM 36-2015 on 4 March 2015.

HELCOM HOD 50-2016, *OUTCOME of the 50th Meeting of the Heads of Delegation*, Agenda Item 4, (4.64).

HELCOM HOD 52-2017, *HELCOM-EUSBSR workshop on internal nutrient reserves*, (3-4), Agenda Item 3.

HELCOM Pressure 6-2017, *A joint HELCOM-EUSBSR workshop on internal nutrient reserves*, (7-10-Rev. 1), Agenda Item 7.

Finnish Authorities

HE 120/2004.

HE 277/2009.

Finnish Legislation

Act on Environmental Impact Assessment Procedure (252/2017) ("Laki ympäristövaikutusten arviointimenettelystä").

COMBATTING EUTROPHICATION IN THE BALTIC SEA 93

Act on the Finnish EEZ (1058/2004) ("Laki Suomen talousvyöhykkeestä").
Act on the Organisation of River Basin Management and the Marine Strategy (1299/2004) ("Laki vesienhoidon ja merenhoidon järjestämisestä").
Act on the Prevention of Marine Pollution (1415/1994) ("Merensuojelulaki").
Environmental Protection Act (527/2014) ("Ympäristönsuojelulaki").
Nature Conservation Act (1096/1996) ("Luonnonsuojelulaki").
Water Act (587/2011) ("Vesilaki").
Waste Act (646/2011) ("Jätelaki").

Swedish Authorities

Havs- och vattenmyndighetens (SwAM) rapport 2015:2, *Havsplanering – nuläge 2014: Statlig planering i territorialhav och ekonomisk zon*, Diarienummer 137-2014, February 2015, [in Swedish].

Swedish Environmental Protection Agency (Naturvårdsverket), Rapport 5999, *Miljöeffekter vid muddring och dumpning: En litteratursammanställning*, October 2009, [in Swedish].

Swedish Environmental Protection Agency (Naturvårdsverket), Report, *Muddring och hantering av muddermassor: Vägledning om tillämpning av 11 och 15 kap Miljöbalken*, Miljörättsavdelningen 2010-02-18, [in Swedish].

Swedish Environmental Protection Agency (Naturvårdsverket), Report 6790, *Swedish Environmental Law – An introduction to the Swedish legal system for environmental protection*, October 2017.

Swedish Legislation

Act on the Continental Shelf (SFS 1966:314) ("Lag om kontinentalsockeln").
Act on Sweden's Exclusive Economic Zone (SFS 1992:1140) ("Lag om Sveriges ekonomiska zon").
Law (SFS 1998:812) with specific rules for water operations (unofficial translation) ("Lag med särskilda bestämmelser om vattenverksamhet").
Ordinance (SFS 2004:660) on Management of Water Quality and Environment (the Water Management Ordinance), ("Förordning om förvaltning av kvaliteten på vattenmiljön").
Ordinance (SFS 2010:1341) on Marine Environment, ("Havsmiljöförordning").
Ordinance (SFS 2013:251) on Environmental Assessment ("Miljöprövningsförordningen").
Swedish Environmental Code (SFS 1998:808) ("Miljöbalken").

Case Law
ICJ

Judgment in the Case Concerning *Pulp Mills on the River Uruguay* (Argentina v. Uruguay) of 20 April, 2010 ICJ Rep 14.

ITLOS

Request for an advisory opinion by Sub-regional fisheries Commission (SFRC), Advisory Opinion, ITLOS, 2015, Case No. 21, available online: https://www.itlos.org/fileadmin/itlos/documents/cases/case_no.21/advisory_opinion_published/2015_21-advop-E.pdf (accessed on 2 August 2019).

Responsibilities and Obligations of States Sponsoring Persons and Entities with Respect to Activities in the Area (Advisory Opinion) [2011] ITLOS Rep 10, Case No. 17.

Southern Bluefin Tuna Cases, (New Zealand v. Japan; Australia v. Japan) Provisional Measures, ITLOS, 1999, Case No. 3 and 4, available online: https://www.itlos.org/fileadmin/itlos/documents/cases/case_no_3_4/published/C34-O-27_aug_99.pdf (accessed on 2 August 2019).

PCA

Chagos Marine Protected Area Arbitration (Mauritius v. United Kingdom) (UNCLOS Annex VII Arbitral tribunal), Permanent Court of Arbitration, 2011, Case 2011-03, available online: www.pcacases.com/pcadocs/MU-UK%2020150318%20Award.pdf (accessed on 24 January 2019).

The Matter of the South China Sea Arbitration (Philippines v. China) (UNCLOS Annex VII Arbitral Tribunal), Permanent Court of Arbitration, 2013, Case 2013-19, available online: https://pcacases.com/web/sendAttach/2086 (accessed on 2 August 2019).

ECJ

C-6/04, *Commission v UK*, ECLI:EU:C:2005:626.

Case C-111/05, *Aktiebolaget NN v. Skatteverket*, ECLI:EU:C:2007:195.

Case C-344/04, *IATA and ELFAA*, ECLI:EU:C:2006:10.

Case C-346/14, *Commission v Republic of Austria*, (Schwarze Sulm), ECLI:EU:C:2016:322.

Case C-461/13, *Bund v. Germany*, (The Weser Case), ECLI:EU:C:2015:433.

Finnish Case Law

KHO 2014:41, ECLI:FI:KHO:2014:41.

Internet Sources

HELCOM action areas [website]: http://www.helcom.fi/action-areas (accessed on 24 January 2019).

Official Finnish legislation [website]: www.finlex.fi (accessed on 10 June 2019).

Miscellaneous / Reports

Common Implementation Strategy for the Water Framework Directive and the Floods Directive, Guidance Doc no 36, *Exemptions to the Environmental Objectives according to Art. 4(7): New modifications to the physical characteristics of surface water bodies, alterations to the level of groundwater, or new sustainable human development activities* – Document endorsed by EU Water Directors at their meeting in Tallinn on 4–5 December 2017.

GESAMP, *High level review of a wide range of proposed marine geoengineering techniques*, Working Group 41, Report of 29 March 2019, available at www.gesamp.org/publi cations/high-level-review-of-a-wide-range-of-proposed-marine-geoengineering -techniques (accessed 2.5.2019).

Hollo, E. J., *Legal Aspects on the Construction of a Gas Pipeline in the EEZ of Finland*, Petition Committee 29th January 2008 (Public Hearing in the European Parliament, Brussels: 2008).

Minutes from the seminar *"Sea-based Measures – to reduce consequences of Eutrophication"*, held at Stockholm University 12 February 2015, and planned jointly with Stockholm University, SWAM and the Swedish Ministry of Environment and Energy.

Proceedings of the 2015 Science Day Symposium on Marine Geoengineering, held on 23 April 2015 at IMO Headquarters, London, United Kingdom.

Rydin, E. and Kumblad, L., *Ecologically relevant phosphorus in coastal sediments*, HELCOM-EUSBSR Workhop in Goteborg 28.–29.11.2017.

Vahanen Environment Oy and Centrum Balticum, *Speeding up the Ecological Recovery of the Baltic Sea* (Ministry of the Environment of Finland, Helsinki: 2018), available online: https://vahanen.com/app/uploads/2018/05/Speeding_up_the_ecological_ recovery_of_the_Baltic_Sea.pdf, (accessed on 10 January 2018).

Authors' Biographical Notes

Henrik Ringbom

Ph.D. (2007), is Professor II at the Scandinavian Institute of Maritime Law at the University of Oslo (Norway), Professor II, KG Jebsen Centre for the Law of the Sea, UiT the Arctic University of Norway (Tromsø, Norway) and Adjunct Professor (Docent) at Åbo Akademi University in Turku/Åbo (Finland). He has published widely in the field of European and international maritime and environmental law and was academically responsible for the legal part of the study for the Finnish Ministry of the Environment on 'Speeding up the Ecological Recovery of the Baltic Sea' (2018).

Brita Bohman

Ph.D. (2017), is post doc researcher in ocean governance law at University of Gothenburg (until 2019) and Senior Lecturer in environmental law at Stockholm University (Sweden). Her Ph.D. thesis, 'Transboundary Law for Social-Ecological Resilience?: A

Study on Eutrophication in the Baltic Sea Area', addressed legal approaches to complex problems such as eutrophication, and she has published a number of papers on the regulation of eutrophication in the Baltic Sea, including co-authorship for the legal part of the study for the Finnish Ministry of the Environment on 'Speeding up the Ecological Recovery of the Baltic Sea' (2018).

Saara Ilvessalo

LL.M. (2016), is the Coordinator of Baltic Area Legal Studies BALEX, a legal competence cluster established by the University of Turku and Åbo Akademi University (Finland). She was co-author and coordinator of the legal part of the study for the Finnish Ministry of the Environment on 'Speeding up the Ecological Recovery of the Baltic Sea' (2018).

Printed in the United States
By Bookmasters